CAMBRIDGE
Lower Secondary
Global Perspectives

Rob Bircher, Mike Gould, Mark Pedroz and Ed Walsh

Series Editor: Mark Pedroz

T0340508

Stage 8: Student's Book

William Collins' dream of knowledge for all began with the publication of his first book in 1819.

A self-educated mill worker, he not only enriched millions of lives, but also founded a flourishing publishing house. Today, staying true to this spirit, Collins books are packed with inspiration, innovation and practical expertise.

They place you at the centre of a world of possibility and give you exactly what you need to explore it.

Collins. Freedom to teach.

Published by Collins

An imprint of HarperCollinsPublishers
The News Building, 1 London Bridge Street, London, SE1 9GF, UK

HarperCollinsPublishers
Macken House, 39/40 Mayor Street Upper, Dublin 1, D01 C9W8, Ireland

Browse the complete Collins catalogue at
www.collins.co.uk

10 9 8 7 6 5 4 3

ISBN 978-0-00-854937-4

British Library Cataloguing-in-Publication Data

A catalogue record for this publication is available from the British Library.

Series editor: Mark Pedroz
Authors: Rob Bircher, Mike Gould, Mark Pedroz and Ed Walsh
Publisher: Elaine Higgleton
Product manager: Catherine Martin
Project manager and development editor: Caroline Low
Copy editor: Susan Ross, Ross Economics and Editorial Services Ltd
Proofreader: Claire Throp
Cover designer: Gordon McGilp
Cover illustrator: Ann Paganuzzi
Internal designer: Ken Vail Graphic Design
Typesetter: David Jimenez
Production controller: Lyndsey Rogers
Printed in India by Multivista Global Pvt. Ltd.

Endorsement indicates that a resource has passed Cambridge International's rigorous quality-assurance process and is suitable to support the delivery of a Cambridge International curriculum framework. However, endorsed resources are not the only suitable materials available to support teaching and learning, and are not essential to be used to achieve the qualification. Resource lists found on the Cambridge International website will include this resource and other endorsed resources.

Any references to assessment and/or assessment preparation are the publisher's interpretation of the curriculum framework requirements. Examiners will not use endorsed resources as a source of material for any assessment set by Cambridge International.

While the publishers have made every attempt to ensure that advice on the qualification and its assessment is accurate, the official curriculum framework, specimen assessment materials and any associated assessment guidance materials produced by the awarding body are the only authoritative source of information and should always be referred to for definitive guidance. Cambridge International recommends that teachers consider using a range of teaching and learning resources based on their own professional judgement of their students' needs.

Cambridge International has not paid for the production of this resource, nor does Cambridge International receive any royalties from its sale. For more information about the endorsement process, please visit www.cambridgeinternational.org/endorsed-resources

Cambridge International copyright material in this publication is reproduced under licence and remains the intellectual property of Cambridge Assessment International Education.

Third-party websites and resources referred to in this publication have not been endorsed by Cambridge Assessment International Education.

MIX
Paper | Supporting responsible forestry
FSC™ C007454
FSC
www.fsc.org

This book is produced from independently certified FSC™ paper to ensure responsible forest management.

For more information visit: www.harpercollins.co.uk/green

Acknowledgements

We are grateful to the following teachers for providing feedback on the Stage 8 Student's Book in development:

Christel Ann M. Labrinao and John Lemuel O. Olita, GO School, Tokyo, Japan; Ms Deepa Maurya, Bombay Cambridge International School, India.

Contents

Introduction: How to use this book

The Collins Stage 8 Student's Book offers an introduction to Cambridge Global Perspectives™ at Lower Secondary level, with rich international texts, data and case studies to stimulate your thinking about contemporary global topics.

The book is organised into seven chapters. Each chapter explores different issues and perspectives that are relevant to one of the syllabus topics. In Stage 8, the topics you will explore are 'Environment, pollution and conservation', 'Climate change, energy and resources', 'Development, trade and aid', 'Migration and urbanisation', 'Change in culture and communities', 'Digital world' and 'Law and criminality'.

Chapter 1 revisits the *reflection* skills which will support you in all the work you do in later chapters to develop the six strands of Global Perspectives.

In Chapter 2, you will learn more about carrying out *research*, framing research questions, testing predictions, *evaluating* sources and recording the findings of your research.

Chapter 3 will help you to *analyse* arguments in more depth, explaining graphical and numerical data and supporting evidence, and *evaluating* how effective and credible the arguments in different sources are.

In Chapter 4, you will develop these skills further by using your *analysis* and *evaluation* skills to make interpretations of an issue, exploring a range of case studies and sources, *evaluating* different perspectives to create your own argument in a final class debate.

Key features of the Student's Book

Chapter 5 will help you improve your *research* and *collaboration* skills, as you take on roles in a team project and present your ideas as a group.

In Chapter 6, you will extend your *research*, *analysis* and *communication* skills, analysing evidence and synthesising different perspectives in writing.

Chapters 2–6 each build to a final task that gives you the opportunity to apply your learning, as you investigate an issue from the chapter in more depth.

Finally, Chapter 7 allows you and your teachers to assess your progress, as you draw together your understanding from earlier chapters to undertake a mini project and write a reflective report. In Stage 8, the focus is on developing your appreciation of different national perspectives on global issues. You will conduct research, engage critically with different national and international perspectives on a global issue and then present arguments on behalf of one nation in a Model United Nations debate, aiming to reach an international resolution.

We hope our resources will support you to build skills that you can use in all the subjects you study at Lower Secondary. We hope, too, that the sources you encounter in the book will inspire you to investigate other global issues – the issues that are most important to you, your school, your culture, your local environment and the nation(s) to which you belong.

Mark Pedroz, Series Editor

The opening page of each chapter summarises the skills, topic and issues to be explored, as well as the final task you will undertake.

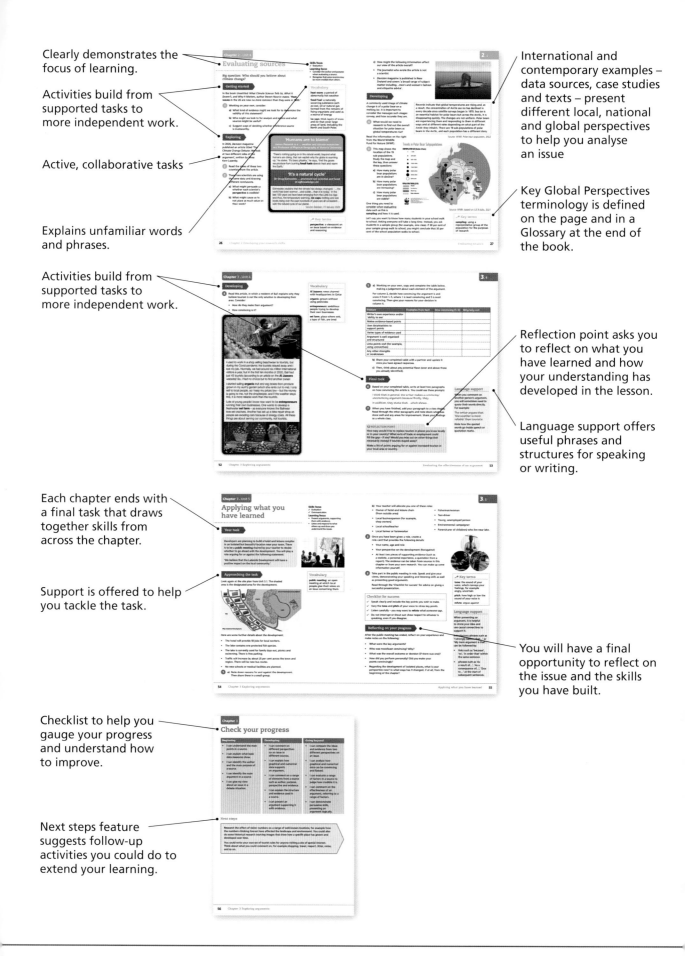

Clearly demonstrates the focus of learning.

Activities build from supported tasks to more independent work.

Active, collaborative tasks

Explains unfamiliar words and phrases.

Activities build from supported tasks to more independent work.

International and contemporary examples – data sources, case studies and texts – present different local, national and global perspectives to help you analyse an issue

Key Global Perspectives terminology is defined on the page and in a Glossary at the end of the book.

Reflection point asks you to reflect on what you have learned and how your understanding has developed in the lesson.

Language support offers useful phrases and structures for speaking or writing.

Each chapter ends with a final task that draws together skills from across the chapter.

Support is offered to help you tackle the task.

You will have a final opportunity to reflect on the issue and the skills you have built.

Checklist to help you gauge your progress and understand how to improve.

Next steps feature suggests follow-up activities you could do to extend your learning.

Developing your reflection skills

Environment, pollution and conservation

Many of us are concerned about the environment – our surroundings, including the air, the land and the water on our planet: the Earth's natural resources. Pollution is when something poisonous or harmful is added into the environment, and unfortunately many human activities are polluting the land, air and water around us locally, nationally and globally. One way of tackling this is conservation, which means protecting areas of the environment from damage by humans.

In this chapter, you will be exploring the topic 'Environment, pollution and conservation', thinking about the following issues:

- **How do we find answers to big questions?**
- **Is there a problem with plastic pollution in our local area?**
- **What is the SMART way to improve?**

You will be developing a range of reflection skills:

1.1 Reflecting on how working together can help answer big questions

1.2 Reflecting on how research can change your perspective

1.3 Reflecting on how you could improve.

Your final task will be to plan and carry out fieldwork in your local area, working as a group. You will also work together to present your research findings.

Reflecting on how working together can help answer big questions

Skills focus
✓ Reflection

Learning focus
- Identify your personal contribution to teamwork.
- Consider the benefits and challenges of teamwork.

Big question: How do we find answers to big questions?

Getting started

1 **a)** Work in a group to create a spider diagram (a mind map) about pollution.

Your diagram should include what you already know about:

- types of pollution (such as water and noise pollution)
- causes of pollution (for example, vehicle emissions)
- impacts of pollution (for example, the effects of pesticides on bees).

Find a way to record how long it took you to complete the task (such as a stopwatch function on a phone).

As you work, come up with a way of making sure you can identify everyone's individual **contributions** to your diagram.

b) When you have finished, multiply the time it took you to complete the task by the number of people in your group.

Is this a fair way to measure how effective teamwork is compared to individual work? Discuss this with the rest of the class.

> **Vocabulary**
>
> **contribution**: the part that someone or something plays in achieving a result or making progress
>
> **marine**: to do with the sea and oceans

In Stage 7 of Global Perspectives, you recorded reflections on working as a group, and considered what could be done to improve your group working skills. You also reflected on all you learned at the end of Stage 7. Have a look back at those reflections now.

Exploring

2 Working on your own, read the list of facts about plastic pollution in the seas.

a) Highlight or note down the statistics – the figures.

b) Which countries or regions do you think are most responsible for plastic pollution in the oceans? Explain your thinking. How might you be able to find out if your theory is right?

Plastic pollution – the facts

- There are currently 165 million tonnes of plastic in the world's oceans; most of which sinks to the ocean floor (only 1 per cent of plastic pollution floats).

- Currently, around 11 million tonnes of plastic enter the oceans every year, out of the 275 million tonnes of global plastic waste that humans create every year.

- Sea creatures get caught in plastic products. One million seabirds and 100,000 **marine** animals are killed because of plastic pollution each year.

- Plastic also breaks down into tiny pieces which marine animals then eat. Plastic absorbs poisons from other pollution, harming the animals that eat the plastic.

Developing

The list above gives big figures for plastic pollution, but how do we know those figures? If you count one number per second, it would still take nearly 12 days to count to a million, so there's no way one person has counted 1 million dead seabirds around the world's oceans, for example.

3 a) In a group, decide how you think the numbers in the list have been arrived at. (Hint: the photos at the top of the next page may help.)

b) Explain why teamwork between pollution scientists would be important in establishing these numbers.

The left image shows students **sampling** sea water at a beach in Brooklyn, New York, USA. The image on the right shows small fragments of plastic, called microplastics, that have been separated from sea water using a sieve.

Marine Pollution Bulletin

Volume 64, Issue 3, March 2012, Pages 653-661

ELSEVIER

Numerical modelling of floating debris in the world's oceans

L.C.-M. Lebreton [a, b], S.D. Greer [a, b], J.C. Borrero [a, b, c] ✉

a ASR Limited Martine Consulting and Research, 1 Wainui Road, Raglan 3225, New Zealand
b SEA·THOS Foundation, 1212 Abbot Kinney Blvd. Suite C, Venice, CA 90291, USA
c University of Southern California, Department of Civil and Environmental Engineering, Los Angeles, CA 90089-2531, USA

Available online 20 January 2012.

Scientists publish 'papers' or articles to tell other people about their research. The scientific paper lists the names of people who wrote the research.

Source: *Marine Pollution Bulletin*, 2012.

Here is an example of the start of a paper about plastic pollution. Can you see where the names of the authors are listed?

Having your name on a scientific paper shows that you made an important contribution to the research. The order of the names is also important: the first name is usually the person who contributed the most to the research; sometimes the last person listed did the most organising.

Science papers often use other people's research and **data** in their work. For example, the paper here used data from 14 expeditions in which sailing boats collected data on marine pollution.

 4 **a)** How do you think the authors of a paper decide who contributed the most to the research? For example, do you think this is based on hours spent in the lab, number of ideas contributed, or most words written?

  b) How do scientific papers acknowledge the contributions of other people to their work?

🔑 Key terms

data: facts and statistics (numerical data) gathered for analysis

You can find out more about the research involved in this scientific paper by searching online for 'The Seas of Plastic Interactive'. The webpage also includes information about which countries or regions are most responsible for plastic pollution in the oceans, to check your answer to question 2b.

Final task

5 Your task, working in a group, is to come up with an answer to this question: 'How many plastic items are thrown away in your school every year?'

Start by making an estimate on your own, then work together following these steps:

a) Count how many plastic items you throw away at school in one day as an individual.

b) In your group or as a class, add all these individual numbers up and divide them by the number of individuals to give you an average per student.

c) Multiply this average by the number of students in your school.

d) Multiply this number by the number of school days in a year.

e) How close was your first estimate to the final number? Was it higher or lower?

6 Working as a group, write a short research paper to share your findings. Your paper should:

• have a suitable title

• explain why it is important to find out about plastic waste

• explain the method you followed to reach your results

• suggest next steps – what could be done with your research data.

Add the names of everyone in your group according to contributions made, with the person who made the biggest contribution first and the person who was most important for organising the work at the end.

❷ REFLECTION POINT

Thinking about the tasks you have completed for this lesson, what are the benefits of teamwork for finding out information? Are there any risks in using lots of people working together to find out information? How easy is it to measure individual contributions to team efforts?

Reflecting on how research can change your perspective

Skills focus
✓ Reflection
Learning focus
• Consider ways that doing research might change your perspective.

Big question: Is there a problem with plastic pollution in our local area?

Getting started

Most plastic pollution reaches the sea because it is **dumped** in rivers or gets washed into rivers. The plastic then gets carried by the rivers into the sea and onto beaches.

1. a) Think about your local area (this could be the school grounds or a larger area). Where does your group think the worst plastic pollution and the least plastic pollution would be?

   To make a group decision about this, follow these steps:

   Step 1: Everyone lists their two sites (most and least polluted).

   Step 2: Compare all the sites as a group.

   Step 3: Use the two sites (most and least polluted) that were listed the most.

   b) As a group, draw a map of your local area and mark these two areas on. Use colours and a **key** to show your choices.

   c) Record your individual view about whether your local area has a problem with plastic pollution or not.

2. Some parts of our local areas are kept clean of plastic pollution.

   a) Where does this happen in your local area?

   b) Who provides this service?

Exploring

3 In your group, you will carry out **fieldwork** on plastic pollution in your local area (this could be the school grounds). Before you set out, you will need to decide:

a) which **sites** you will **survey** as a class – you will need to cover the best and worst areas that each group identified from the 'Getting started' activity, and each site will need its own number

b) how many sites your group will survey – different groups can survey the same site, but ideally the class will collectively survey more than two sites

c) how you will measure the extent of plastic pollution in each location – this will need to be done in the same way for each group so that your results are consistent. That way your fieldwork data can be **collated**.

A good way to make sure each group measures and records in the same way is to copy and complete a record sheet like this one.

Plastic pollution fieldwork – record sheet

Group name: _Group Amazing!_

Date and time: _16 June, 14:15_

Site number: _4_

Types of plastic pollution	Amount of plastic pollution	Notes
Plastic bags	||| (3)	
Crisp packets	‖‖‖ (5)	
Cling film / wrapping			Still had a sandwich inside
Drinks bottles	|| (2)	
Bottle tops	‖‖‖ ||| (8)	
Takeaway food boxes	|| (2)	

Date and time: _____

Site number: _____

Types of plastic pollution	Amount of plastic pollution	Notes

Use the 'Checklist for success' to help you work effectively together as a team.

Checklist for success

✔ Agree on the project objective – what are you all working to achieve?

✔ Decide on roles – for example, researcher, illustrator, checker, project manager.

✔ Make sure everyone knows how their role delivers the project objective.

✔ Think about which group work skills you are looking to improve as a team and individually.

Vocabulary

site: a particular place or area

All fieldwork needs to be **risk** assessed. This means thinking about:

- the **hazards** that might be involved in carrying out the fieldwork

- how likely those hazards are to happen (risk)

- what could be done to reduce these risks.

For example, there might be a moderate risk of road traffic hazards in some locations. Risk could be reduced by making sure groups always stand as far back from the road as possible, and by wearing high visibility clothing.

4 Your teacher will risk assess your fieldwork using official school risk assessment procedures. However, you should also think as a group about:

- what the hazards involved in the fieldwork might be

- how the risk of these hazards occurring can be reduced.

As a group, complete a chart like this one, adding the hazards that relate to your fieldwork sites, deciding on their risk, and then working together to agree the actions in the last two columns.

Developing

5 When you have safely completed your fieldwork, the next task is to analyse and present your results. The aim is to produce a class map of the area you surveyed, which shows the level of plastic pollution at each site that was surveyed.

For this to work:

- Each group needs to present its data in the same way as every other group.

- Each group can then add its data presentation to the map.

- Each group can then compare the class results with its original ideas about where the most and least pollution would be.

(L = Low, M = Medium, H = High)

Hazard	How likely is it to occur?	What action should be taken to reduce the risk?	What action should be taken if the hazard occurs?
Rainfall	H	Students should bring suitable clothing (raincoats)	If rainfall is very heavy, students should return to school
Cold conditions			
Sunburn			
Heat stroke or heat exhaustion			
Slips or trips on uneven surfaces			
Hazardous substances			
Traffic hazards			
Causing offence or inconvenience to members of the public			
Getting lost			

Here is how one class presented their results:

- First, they marked in their sites on an online map of the area.

- Then they used a spreadsheet app to produce graphs of their findings, which they pasted onto the map.

- The results showed the average for each site – if more than one group had surveyed the same site, the groups' results were added together and then divided by the number of groups.

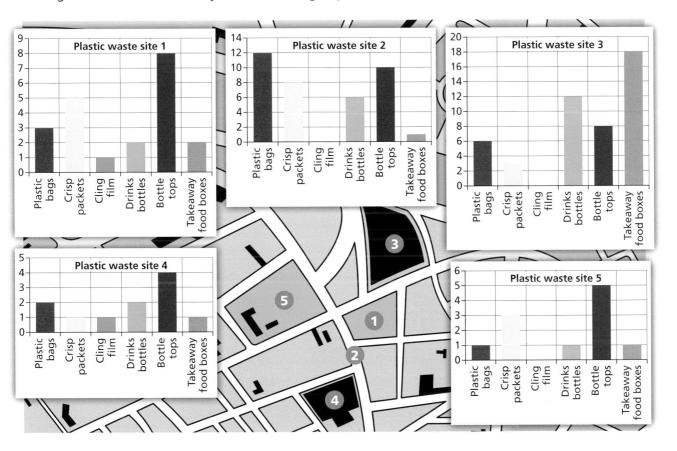

Final task

6 Looking at the class map of plastic pollution in your local area, think about solutions to the problem of plastic pollution.

Working on your own, write an email to the person responsible for waste collection and disposal in your local area. The email should:

a) introduce yourself and explain why you are writing

b) describe the survey of plastic pollution you carried out and your research findings

c) explain what you think could be done to reduce the amount of plastic pollution in specific problem areas

d) conclude by expressing why it is important to reduce the amount of plastic pollution.

❓ REFLECTION POINT

How did the experience of carrying out fieldwork affect your ideas about whether plastic pollution is a problem in your local area? Did any of your expectations turn out to be different from the results of your fieldwork?

Discuss your reflections with others in your group. Make a note of any changes in your perspectives on plastic pollution in your local area.

Reflecting on how you could improve

Skills focus
✓ Reflection
Learning focus
• Identify what you've learned.
• Make a link to something you want to improve.

Big question: What is the SMART way to improve?

Getting started

1 What can you improve about your own contribution to plastic pollution?

a) Answer these questions about your own use of plastics. For each question, say whether you always do this, sometimes do this, or rarely or never do this. Draw up a table like this one to use for your answers.

	Always do this (✓)	Sometimes do this (✓)	Rarely or never do this (✓)
1. I have a reusable bottle that I use for water.			
2. I have a reusable cup that I use when buying hot drinks or smoothies.			
3. I refuse plastic straws for drinks.			
4. I buy things with as little packaging as possible.			
5. I refuse disposable plastic cutlery.			
6. I carry a reusable shopping bag.			
7. I use reusable wraps to wrap up food in packed lunches.			
8. I recycle as much of my plastic waste as I can.			
9. I reuse plastic containers whenever I can.			
10. I tell other people how they can reduce plastic pollution.			

b) Most of us probably don't do as much as we could to reduce our own contribution to plastic pollution. Use your answers to part a) to identify some areas where you could do a little more.

c) Set yourself a target for ways in which you will improve. Write your targets down. For example, 'I will bring a reusable water bottle to school every day for one week.'

Exploring

2 What skills would you like to improve as a
school learner?

a) List up to 10 skills you think are important for
school learning. Your list of skills may well be
different from others because we all learn in
different ways.

b) For each one, decide if you are just getting started with this
skill, are nearly there or are confident using it. You could do
this in a table like the one you did for plastics.

- Ask for help when I need it.
- Be more organised about homework.
- Listen more in class.
- Ask more questions.
- Think about what I've learned.

Developing

3 Lots of schools and businesses use SMART targets to help
people improve.

SMART targets are Specific, Measurable, Achievable, Relevant
and Time-bound:

Specific → Focused, not vague: you identify something definite you want to improve.

Measurable → There is always a way to measure progress.

Achievable → It is possible to meet the target in the time available.

Relevant → The target is relevant to you and your goals.

Time-bound → Say when you will aim to achieve the target by.

a) Try writing a SMART target for something you want to
improve about your learning skills – or you could write more
than one target.

b) Talk to a partner about the target and ask them to help you
check if it is SMART.

Do you remember what
you learned about SMART
targets from Stage 7?

Final task

4 As a group, think about the challenges of working as a team.

a) What challenges have you faced when working together?

b) How could you improve the way you work together as a
team to reduce those challenges?

c) Write some SMART targets to support your improvement as
a team.

? REFLECTION POINT
How would you advise
the global community to
work together to stop
plastic pollution?

Check your progress

Beginning	Developing	Going beyond
• I can show my own contribution to teamwork.	• I can talk about what my contribution has added to teamwork.	• I can talk about my own contribution to teamwork and how I could improve it.
• I can say how working together helps achieve a goal.	• I can describe the benefits and challenges of working together to achieve a goal.	• I can discuss the benefits and challenges of working together to achieve a goal in general and from my own experience.
• I can talk about what I've learned from an activity and whether my views have changed.	• I can discuss ways that my ideas may be influenced by new information or the ideas of others.	• I can explain ways in which my ideas about an issue have changed because of research I did or from exploring other people's perspectives.
• I can say what sort of activities help me learn best.	• I can identify what skills I've learned or improved from doing an activity.	• I can identify what skills I've learned or improved from doing an activity and relate those to my own strengths as a learner and to ways of improving even more.

Next steps

Find out whether there are any groups in your local area that work to reduce plastic pollution. If there are no groups, perhaps you could help to start one.

Explore other ways of measuring pollution in your local area. For example, you could research how to make a device to measure the particles carried in air pollution – and analyse those particles with a school microscope.

Do some secondary research to find out more about global plastic pollution. The Seas of Plastic Interactive webpage (see Unit 1.1) is a good place to start.

Developing your research skills

Climate change, energy and resources

Some days it may seem that the news is full of stories about the latest environmental challenges facing us. Issues arise due to our demand for energy and our use of the Earth's natural resources, both of which can damage the environment and make our climate more extreme. To understand and meet these challenges, we need to focus on the right questions.

In this chapter, you will be exploring the topic of 'Climate change, energy and resources', thinking about the following issues:

- **Could your school be self-sufficient in energy?**
- **Does it benefit an area to be rich in natural resources?**
- **Could your school manage its waste better?**
- **Who should you believe about climate change?**
- **How can you reduce your carbon footprint?**

You will be developing a range of research and evaluation skills:

2.1 Constructing relevant research questions

2.2 Using sources to answer research questions

2.3 Using research to test predictions and answer research questions

2.4 Evaluating sources

2.5 Recording research findings

2.6 Applying what you have learned.

Your final task will be to prepare a presentation about how your school could become more sustainable and how you could persuade people of the merits of this.

Constructing relevant research questions

Skills focus
✓ Research

Learning focus
- Identify relevant questions around an area of study.
- Select a single research question to guide an investigation.

Big question: Could your school be self-sufficient in energy?

Vocabulary

self-sufficient: not reliant on others; in the context of energy, it means not using up more energy than you produce

consumption: to use up a resource – here, energy

transfers: movement from one place to another

generator: a machine that changes mechanical energy into electricity

Getting started

1 Imagine your school has been told that it must become **self-sufficient** in energy as part of a government drive to reduce energy **consumption** and save money.

  a) What do you know about your school's current energy use?

  b) How do you think your school could become more energy self-sufficient?

Exploring

The Sankey diagram is a useful way of looking at the **transfers** of energy in and out of a system, such as a school.

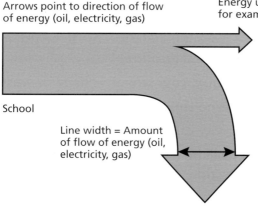

Arrows point to direction of flow of energy (oil, electricity, gas)

Energy used by school that has a useful effect, for example heating, lighting

Energy supplied to school, for example oil, electricity, gas – this is the input (what goes in) to the system

School

Line width = Amount of flow of energy (oil, electricity, gas)

Energy released in ways that isn't useful, for example heat from lights, sound from air-conditioning units

2 Using the Sankey diagram and thinking about the school as an energy system, what could you ask about:

- the energy supplied to the school
- the purposes that energy is put to
- how energy efficient the school is?

  a) Working with a partner, come up with and note down questions to ask for each area.

  b) Join with another pair and compare questions. Decide which are the most important questions.

In this unit, you will be looking at how to use questions to focus your research. So, what makes a good research question? Here are three ideas:

- *The question can be answered objectively.* 'What's the best colour for a mobile phone?' is not a good research question because the responses will be personal and subjective. 'Which colours of mobile phones are more popular?' is a better research question because you can gather data that shows preferences regardless of personal choice.

- *It can be answered by collecting or using information.* 'If I toss a coin, which way up will it land?' is not a good research question because we cannot know this (in advance), but 'What is the probability of a coin landing a certain way?' is a better research question because the data could be gathered.

- *It hasn't yet been answered.* 'What is the chemical composition of chocolate?' is not a good research question because it's already known, but 'Is the water in the local stream drinkable?' is a better question because it may not be known.

3 Return to your list of important questions. In your original pair:

    a) Decide whether they are good research questions. Can you improve them?

    b) What did you need to change?

Developing

You are now going to find out about three aspects of energy:

- How we produce energy (how it is supplied to us)

- How we use, or consume, energy

- How much of the energy we use is wasted.

4 Read through the information below. If your school was being offered these six pieces of equipment, what questions would you want to ask before deciding which to purchase and install?

    a) A wind **generator** could be built in the school grounds. When the wind blows, it turns the blades and powers a generator, which produces electricity.

    b) Solar cells could be placed on the ground or the roof. When the sun shines, these transfer energy from sunlight into electricity.

c) Bio-digestors are supplied with organic waste such as plant material. As the material **decomposes**, it produces methane gas, which can be burned as a fuel.

d) Ground source heat pumps extract **thermal energy** from under the ground, which can be used for heating.

e) Storage batteries store electricity until it is needed. They are used with equipment such as wind generators and solar cells so that there can still be a supply of energy even if there is no wind or sun.

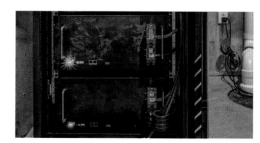

f) Solar panels can be installed on the roof. They have water flowing through them which is then heated by the sun. The hot water can be used for heating and cooking.

Now let's think about energy use or consumption. You probably don't know everything about how energy is being used in your school. If much of the consumption is for appliances that need electricity, then being self-sufficient will mean finding different ways of supplying that electricity. If the energy is used for heating or hot water, then other solutions might be better.

5 Design a questionnaire to use with teachers and other staff to find out what they use energy for in school. Your questionnaire will need to include a way of recording the amount of energy used – for example, whether an electrical appliance is used only occasionally or every day.

Vocabulary

decomposes: rots, breaks down

thermal energy: the energy contained in a material; the amount depends on the temperature of the material and its state (solid, liquid or gas)

insulator: a substance that is a poor conductor of heat

You may want to revisit your work from Stage 7 on how to create questionnaires.

Finally, let's look at energy efficiency.

Imagine you go to a school in a hot country where a key priority is keeping the classrooms cool. The school has large windows to let in light, but on sunny days the rooms get too hot. The current solution is to run an air-conditioning unit, but this uses a lot of electricity – so you are looking to find a different solution.

Here are three possible solutions:

1. Blinds can be closed when the sun gets too hot. They put the room in shade.	2. Double glazing is two layers of glass window with air trapped between them. The air acts as an **insulator**.	3. Some of the existing window area could be replaced with solid walls to reduce the area of glass.

6 **a)** Working with a partner, come up with questions to research each of these approaches.

b) Share your ideas with another pair and refine the questions.

Final task

7 You have been asked to speak to the school leadership team about how your school could be more energy self-sufficient. They want to know what important questions they should be asking.

Working in a small group, design a poster or set of slides that answers these questions:

a) Indicate the aspects of energy self-sufficiency the school should consider.

b) For each of these aspects, identify the key questions to ask.

c) Explain why asking those questions will help the school become more energy self-sufficient.

❓ REFLECTION POINT

Think about your experience in this unit of designing good research questions.

- How easy was it to construct good research questions?

- Look back at the ideas about what makes a good research question. Which aspects of these did you find trickier and why?

Using sources to answer research questions

Skills focus
✓ Research

Learning focus
- Use sources to locate relevant information.
- Reference sources effectively.
- Answer research questions.

Big question: Does it benefit an area to be rich in natural resources?

Getting started

1 Imagine that **deposits** of a **precious metal** used in the manufacture of mobile phones have been found in your area. Working with a partner, discuss these questions:

a) How might this benefit your area?

b) How might this cause problems?

c) How could you find out the likely impacts of the discovery on your area?

Exploring

Cornwall, in the south-west of England, is an area rich in **minerals**, including copper, lead and tin. In the early part of the 19th century, it was one of the richest mining areas in the world and had hundreds of mines going deep underground, employing thousands of people.

The photograph shows the mining area at Dolcoath, near the town of Redruth, in 1900. It is covered with mine workings, there are many **shafts** running underground, and the land is taken up with buildings and piles of waste from mine workings.

> **Vocabulary**
>
> **deposits**: concentrations of minerals in the Earth's crust
>
> **precious metal**: a valuable metal such as gold or silver
>
> **minerals**: a single element, such as copper or tin, or a compound, such as salt or quartz, occurring naturally in a pure form
>
> **shafts**: long tunnels built by miners to give access to minerals below ground
>
> **furnishings**: furniture, curtains and carpets
>
> **illiterate**: unable to read or write

Dolcoath Mine, Cornwall, in 1900.

Mining made Cornwall a wealthy place. Grand houses were built and shops in towns such as Redruth sold fine clothes and **furnishings**.

The main street in Redruth, Cornwall, in 1898.

You are going to research copper, lead and tin mining in Cornwall in the 19th century.

2 **a)** Using the internet, explore these questions with a partner. Jot down some notes.

- Why were copper, lead and tin so valuable in the 19th century?

- What was life like for the miners extracting these metals?

- How well distributed was the wealth?

b) Compare notes with another pair. Focus on the sources you found. How useful were they?

When you use existing sources of evidence (secondary research), you need to clearly reference the material. This is important because:

- It provides evidence, which makes your assertions more persuasive

- It supports your work, especially if the sources quoted are reputable, showing that other people agree with you

- It credits the author or researcher, acknowledging their work (and not falsely suggesting that it is your work).

To reference an internet source, the title of the item should be quoted, along with the address of the web page – the URL. (The URL is found at the top of your web browser when you are looking at the article; it can be copied and pasted into your work.)

Here's an example of a style you could use:

> National Trust (2022) Ten things you probably didn't know about Cornish mining [Online] 29 July 2022. Available from: https://www.nationaltrust.org.uk/lists/ten-things-you-probably-didnt-know-about-cornish-mining [Accessed 18 August 2022]

3 Discuss these questions in a small group:

a) China clay was also mined in Cornwall – and still is. Why is it important to focus on copper, lead and tin when answering question 2?

b) Many of the miners in the early 19th century were **illiterate**. Why might it be difficult to find out what their life was like?

c) The photographs on pages 18 and 19 were taken in the late 19th and early 20th centuries. Why can we not refer to photographs from the early 19th century?

d) What do your answers to the above three questions reveal about the limitations of using sources?

Miners working in Dolcoath Mine, 1893.

Mining can be dirty and dangerous work. Child labour was common in 19th-century Britain, with boys as young as 10 working in the mines. There were frequent accidents, and many people were injured or killed when mines collapsed.

Mining in Cornwall has scarred the landscape. The metals extracted came out of the ground as **metal ores**. An ore is a rock that contains metal but also contains other substances, which need to be separated. This often leaves waste products. In Cornwall, these waste products were left in piles on the land. The chemicals they contained meant that little or no vegetation would grow on the land where they were dumped.

The mining industry depends upon the **market price** of the products, and this can vary a lot. If the market price falls too low, mines can suddenly close down overnight.

Cornwall is now one of the poorest parts of Britain, having a Gross Valued Added (GVA) of 70.9% of the national average. No copper, lead or tin has been mined for many years, and many parts of the local landscape still show the scars of mineral waste and **contamination**.

4 Working with a partner, research these questions and make notes, including a record of sources used:

a) Find out what GVA means and explain it in simple terms.

b) Why did an area made so rich by metal extraction then become so poor?

c) Phytoremediation might be of interest in old mining areas in Cornwall or elsewhere. How could it help Cornwall?

Vocabulary

metal ore: rock that contains a valuable mineral that can be extracted

market price: the current price that is paid for a product

contamination: where something is made harmful or polluted

geothermal fluids: fluids such as water that are naturally heated up inside the earth

Final task

Cornwall may yet return to mining metals. It has deposits of lithium, which is in demand because of its use in electric vehicle batteries. The value of lithium is rising.

Lithium is extracted from the ground by pumping **geothermal fluids** to the surface, removing the lithium and then returning the fluids to the ground. There is hope that such an industry could bring wealth back to Cornwall.

Each Tesla Model S has an estimated 63 kg of lithium in the car battery.

Solar panels are often used to supply power to lithium batteries.

5 Working with a partner, research:

a) where lithium is mined and the current issues with mining for it in the place closest to you

b) how the market price of lithium is changing

c) why those promoting lithium mining are enthusiastic about it

d) issues that have arisen in lithium mining in other countries.

6 Think about what you've learned about the mining history of Cornwall.

a) Why do you think some people in Cornwall might be enthusiastic about lithium mining?

b) Why do you think they might be cautious?

c) Which reference materials have particularly informed and influenced you in answering these last two questions?

❓ REFLECTION POINT

To answer the questions in this unit, you needed to find and use several secondary sources.

- What did you find straightforward about finding suitable reference sources?

- What did you struggle with?

- What advice would you give to someone about good ways of using reference sources to answer research questions?

Using research to test predictions and answer research questions

Skills focus
✓ Research
Learning focus
• Select an appropriate method to carry out research.
• Use research to test predictions and answer research questions.

Big question: Could your school manage its waste better?

Getting started

Waste is often **disposed of** in **landfill sites**. The material sometimes takes many years to decompose and some waste releases dangerous chemicals when it breaks down. Many countries agree that the reduction of landfill waste is a major priority.

1 Think about your school's waste. In a small group, discuss these questions:

a) What waste does your school send to a landfill site?

b) What waste does it recycle?

c) How good do you think your school is at limiting the waste it sends to landfill?

d) How could you gather evidence to find out?

e) Why might this evidence be useful?

Vocabulary

disposed of: got rid of as unwanted

landfill site: an area of land where rubbish is dumped

Exploring

One approach to waste management is 'reduce, re-use, recycle'. Any activity is reviewed by asking these three questions:

• Can we reduce the amount used? For example, can we reduce the number of paper towels used in the washrooms?

• Can we reuse materials? For example, if cooking oil is supplied in bottles, can the used bottles be refilled instead of new bottles being supplied?

• Can we recycle the material? For example, used tyres can be shredded to make a ground cover material where people are learning how to ride horses.

REDUCE **REUSE** **RECYCLE**

2 Working with a partner, find an area of waste management within the school that could be improved such as lightbulbs, food waste, used pens, food packaging or paper waste.

a) Start by researching how your chosen type of waste is disposed of. For example, you could observe what waste is in bins or talk to staff in the school.

b) Design a questionnaire to target key members of the school community (students, teaching staff, and so on).

c) Suggest a target for your school for your chosen type of waste. For example, what could your school do to reduce the amount of that type of waste going to landfill sites?

Managing waste effectively often means changing people's behaviour. If people are used to throwing things away, they may have to think and act differently. They may need to learn to:

- reduce consumption – for example, reading something onscreen rather than printing it

- find ways of extending the life of something – for example, refilling a shampoo bottle rather than throwing it away

- recycle materials that are beyond repair – for example, sending certain materials such as glass and metals to be **reprocessed**.

A customer in an eco shop refills their own container.

3 Working in your group, predict how much you can change people's behaviour regarding the one aspect of waste management you have identified.

a) Record your prediction.

b) Decide how you will measure it. How could you identify an improvement?

c) Write a target about what your school could achieve in 12 months' time.

Developing

Some people think we should add three more actions to 'reduce, reuse, recycle':

• Refuse – you may be offered something that you don't need. For example, people buying coffee may take their own cup rather than use a disposable one.

• Repair – some items could be mended and reused, such as mobile phones, clothes and bicycles.

• Rot – some materials will decompose to make a medium for plants to grow in.

4 Working in a small group, research instances of 'refuse, repair and rot'.

a) Think about examples of materials you could refuse – try not only to find examples but also how common they are.

b) Gather some examples of repairing items – think of ways of saving items from being thrown out.

c) Find out about rotting – research what will rot down well, how the material can then be used and what will grow well in it.

d) Finally, consider how your findings could form part of a promotional campaign in your school.

5 Refer back to the research you did in question 2 and see if any of these three approaches to waste management can be applied to the example you were exploring. Make notes about how this might be done.

6 Some countries have tried to solve the problem of waste management by sending their waste to other countries.

• People in favour of this argue that paying another country to take their waste helps that country's economy and creates jobs.

• People against this argue that the countries that do this will never learn how to manage their waste.

What do you think, and why?

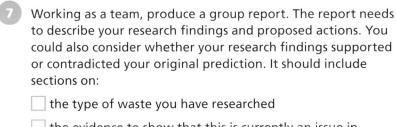

Final task

7 Working as a team, produce a group report. The report needs to describe your research findings and proposed actions. You could also consider whether your research findings supported or contradicted your original prediction. It should include sections on:

☐ the type of waste you have researched

☐ the evidence to show that this is currently an issue in the school

☐ ways you have researched of managing this type of waste more effectively

☐ targets you feel are appropriate for the school

☐ how you have promoted this campaign

☐ a conclusion, indicating the success this has achieved in terms of:

- waste reduction
- increased awareness of the issue.

When writing the conclusion, it is important that you compare your targets with what happened (what was achieved).

❓ REFLECTION POINT

Sometimes the evidence you gathered will be quantitative, where you were able to use numbers to indicate the scale of something. This might apply to the amount of waste, for example.

On other occasions, your research will be qualitative, where you have described something. When you are looking at awareness, this might be qualitative (though it could be quantitative if you asked people questions that could be scored).

Working on your own, look back at the work you did in this unit and suggest:

- one example of quantitative research you did
- one example of qualitative research you did
- why you might sometimes need to do one type and sometimes the other.

Evaluating sources

Skills focus
✓ Evaluation
Learning focus
- Consider the author and purpose when evaluating a source.
- Recognise that some sources may be more credible than others.

Big question: Who should you believe about climate change?

Getting started

In the book *Unsettled: What Climate Science Tells Us, What It Doesn't, and Why It Matters,* author Steven Koonin states: '**Heat waves** in the US are now *no more common* than they were in 1900.'

1. Working on your own, consider:

   a) What kind of evidence might we look for to determine the validity of this statement?

   b) Who might we look to for analysis and advice and what sources might be useful?

   c) Suggest ways of deciding whether a reference source is trustworthy.

Vocabulary

heat wave: a period of abnormally hot weather

fossil fuel: a naturally occurring substance such as coal, oil or natural gas formed from the remains of living organisms and used as a source of energy

ice caps: thick layers of snow and ice that cover large areas of land, including the North and South Poles

Exploring

In 2020, *Denizen* magazine published an article titled 'The Climate Change Debate: We look at two different sides of the argument', written by Mina Kerr-Lazenby.

2. Read the views of these two scientists from the article.

3. These two scientists are using the same data and drawing different conclusions.

   a) What might persuade us whether each scientist's **perspective** is credible?

   b) What might cause us to not place as much value on their work?

'Humans are to blame'

James Renwick is a ... weather and climate researcher and Professor of Physical Geography at Victoria University

'There's nothing going on in the natural world, beyond what humans are doing, that can explain why the globe is warming up,' he states. 'It's basic physics,' he says, 'that the gases we produce from burning **fossil fuels** absorb heat and warm the Earth.'

'It's a natural cycle'

Dr Doug Edmeades ... prominent soil scientist and head of agKnowledge Ltd

Edmeades explains that the climate has always changed. '...the world has been warmer...and colder...than it is today.' In the last 100 years we have been emerging from the Little Ice Age and thus, the temperature warming, **ice caps** melting and sea levels rising over the past hundreds of years are all consistent... with the natural cycle of our planet.

Source: *Denizen*, 23 January 2020.

🔑 Key terms

perspective: a viewpoint on an issue based on evidence and reasoning

c) How might the following information affect our view of the article overall?

- The journalist who wrote the article is not a scientist.

- *Denizen* magazine is published in New Zealand and covers 'a broad range of subject matter including…men's and women's fashion and etiquette advice'.

Developing

A commonly used image of climate change is of a polar bear on melting ice. It is important to consider the messages such images convey, and how accurate they are.

4 What would we need to research to find out the overall situation for polar bears as global temperatures rise?

Read the information on the right from the World Wildlife Fund for Nature (WWF).

5 This map shows the location of the 19 sub-populations. Study the map and the key, then answer these questions.

a) How many polar bear populations are in decline?

b) How many polar bear populations are increasing?

c) How many polar bear populations are stable?

One thing you need to consider when evaluating data such as this is **sampling** and how it is used.

Records indicate that global temperatures are rising and, as a result, the concentration of Arctic sea ice has declined in every decade since satellite surveys began in 1979. Sea ice is an essential habitat for polar bears but across the Arctic, it is disappearing quickly. The changes are not uniform. Polar bears are experiencing them and responding to them in different ways and at different rates depending on what part of the Arctic they inhabit. There are 19 sub-populations of polar bears in the Arctic, and each population has a different story.

Source: WWF, Polar bear population, 2022

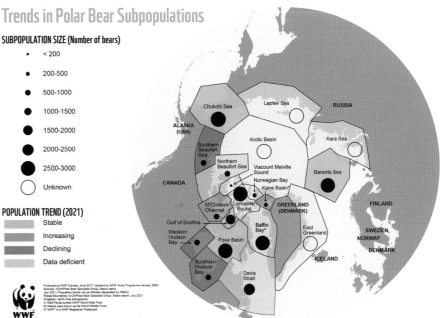

Source: WWF, based on IUCN data, 2021

Let's say you want to know how many students in your school walk to school. Asking everyone will take a long time. Instead, you ask students in a sample group (for example, one class). If 30 per cent of your sample group walk to school, you might conclude that 30 per cent of the school population walks to school.

✐ Key terms

sampling: using a representative group of the population for the purposes of research

However, this approach only works if your sample is **representative** – the sample needs to have the same features as the whole group. So, if your sample is mainly older students, it's less likely that the figures would be representative of the whole school. Older students may be more likely to walk to school than younger ones, for example.

The natural habitat of polar bears is in a very remote and inaccessible part of the world and they are widely distributed in those areas. It is therefore difficult and expensive to get good estimates of their total numbers. However, researchers have realised that studying the changing nature of the ice can also help them identify risks to the bears' numbers.

6 Scientists have to use sampling to make their estimates of polar bear populations.

a) If the data is based on sampling, should we be wary about how accurate it is?

b) An organisation dedicated to the protection of polar bears could spend more of its finances on gathering more data, so that the sample sizes were greater, for example. Suggest reasons for and against the organisation doing this.

If data are used to support an argument in a source you are evaluating, you need to think about how the data are being presented and why.

These two sources present different arguments about changes in the population of polar bears.

7 Work with a partner to discuss and make notes in response to the following questions.

a) Summarise in no more than two sentences the argument that each source is making about polar bear populations.

b) The FEE's article combines the numbers from each of the polar bear populations to produce overall totals. Suggest why the FEE chooses to present the data in terms of the total polar bear population.

Source 1: Polar Bears International (PBI) website – accessed 11.11.22

Conservation Concerns: Climate Warning

Polar bears rely on sea ice to hunt, breed, roam, and sometimes to den. But the Arctic is warming and ice is melting due to human-caused climate change. Already, in parts of the Arctic, longer ice-free seasons and longer fasting periods have led to a decline in some polar bear populations.

Research shows that without action to greatly reduce carbon emissions and stabilize our climate, we could lose all but a few polar bear populations by the end of the century.

Status: Are Polar Bears Endangered?

Because of the expense and logistical difficulties of working in many Arctic locations, there are very few long-term studies of polar bear populations. But those with long-term data sets allow scientists to track changes over time. For example, in **Canada's Western Hudson Bay population**, based on an aerial survey [by the Government of Nunavut] in 2021, the population dropped by 27 per cent in just five years, from 842 bears to 618, continuing the declining trend of the past 30 years. Previous aerial surveys showed a drop of 11 per cent from 2011 to 2016. The population estimate is now roughly half of what it was in the 1980s, when studies using a different technique showed 1200 bears.

Source 2: 'The Myth that the Polar Bear Population is Declining'

2019 article by The Foundation for Economic Education (FEE)

Data from conservation groups and the government show that the polar bear population is roughly five times what it was in the 1950s and three or four times what it was in the 1970s when polar bears became protected under international treaty. In fact […] the polar bear population has been stable for the last three decades.

The health of the polar bear population runs counter to predictions from scholars who have said two-thirds of polar bears will disappear in coming decades because of warming temperatures and melting sea ice in the Arctic.

c) Suggest why the PBI and the WWF focus on polar bear numbers in the constituent sub-populations.

d) Explain how the same sets of data can be used to support two different arguments.

It's important when evaluating a source to consider the nature of the organisation that produced it. Here is how the PBI and the FEE describe themselves on their websites.

'Polar Bears International is made up of a passionate team of conservationists, scientists, and volunteers – working to secure a future for polar bears across the Arctic.'

8 We can see from these descriptions that the FEE has a very different role to the PBI.

a) Why might an organisation dedicated to 'limited government' be keen to suggest there isn't a problem to solve?

b) Why might an organisation like Polar Bears International make a different argument?

c) See what else you can find out about each organisation. Does this additional information encourage you to think that the organisation is a credible source?

Final task

One widely promoted solution to tackle climate change is to encourage people to switch to electric vehicles, so reducing **exhaust emissions**.

9 Research the following points with a partner. For each point, aim to find at least two sources with differing viewpoints.

a) Electric vehicles don't burn fossil fuels, so they reduce emissions of greenhouse gases.

b) The reduction of greenhouse gas emissions by electric vehicles depends on how the electricity used to charge them up has been generated.

c) The environmental impact of a vehicle depends on how it has been manufactured as well as on the fuel it uses.

For each source you find, comment on the credibility of both the author and the publication. Use the 'Checklist for success' to help you.

Checklist for success

Sources can be considered credible when:

- ✔ the source of the evidence is clear
- ✔ the evidence is presented in a fair and neutral way
- ✔ the source is trustworthy and has a good track record
- ✔ the ideas offered are supported by other sources.

'FEE's mission is to inspire, educate, and connect future leaders with the economic, ethical, and legal principles of a free society. These principles include: individual liberty, free-market economics, entrepreneurship, private property, high moral character, and limited government.'

🔑 Key terms

representative: a small group that is typical of members of the whole group

Vocabulary

exhaust emissions: gases and particles that come out of the exhaust (tail pipe) of a petrol- or diesel-fuelled vehicle

❓ REFLECTION POINT

- What tips would you recommend as good ways of establishing the credibility of a source?

- What might cause you to view a source as being less credible?

- How might identifying the credibility of a source change your view about the points being made in an article?

Recording research findings

Skills focus
✓ Research
Learning focus
- Use a range of sources to access relevant information.
- Organise and record findings from primary research.

Big question: How can you reduce your carbon footprint?

Getting started

Have you ever thought about how you could reduce your carbon footprint? Your carbon footprint is the negative impact on the planet caused by the release of **carbon emissions** from your daily activities. We use the term footprint because it indicates the mark on the world you leave behind – and not in a good way.

1 a) Working with a partner, list the things you do that contribute towards your carbon footprint.

   b) Suggest which of these it might be possible to reduce – and how.

   c) What would you need to find out to be able to reduce them?

Exploring

There are many things that contribute to your carbon footprint, so you might be surprised to learn what it is that you can do to make a difference.

There are several different websites that can help you assess your carbon footprint. Simply input a term such as 'measure carbon footprint' into the search engine to access such a resource. This will then ask you questions about your lifestyle and indicate what your carbon footprint is. It may also suggest ways of reducing it.

2 Find different sites to assess your carbon footprint and try them out. By using several (at least three), you will see what aspects of your activities they are asking about – and if they offer similar advice!

   Record the sites you use, and the key points they give you about how to reduce your carbon footprint.

> **Vocabulary**
>
> **carbon emission**: the release of carbon dioxide into the atmosphere

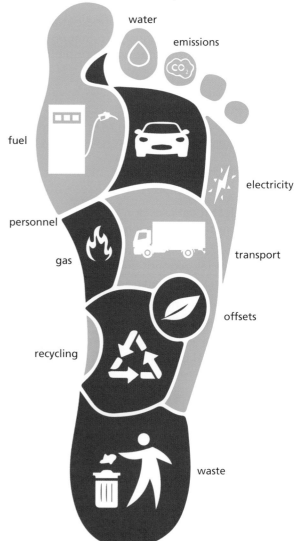

the carbon footprint

water

emissions

fuel

electricity

personnel

gas

transport

offsets

recycling

waste

Many different factors contribute to your carbon footprint. You are now going to explore one of these.

3 Work as a group to design a questionnaire to gather evidence to see what the potential is among class members for reducing their carbon footprint.

a) Start by considering which of these aspects to explore further:

- how people travel around

- how they heat or cool their home

- how much they use home appliances such as a washing machine, tumble dryer or dishwasher

- how many baths or showers they take in a week

- how they cook – and how often

- how they boil water for cooking or drinks – and how often

- how often they eat meat or fish, or foods from abroad

- how much time they spend using their mobile phone – and charging it up

- how much time they spend watching television – and streaming.

b) Identify the key questions to ask in your survey. Remember you will be asking everyone in your class and different people may live in very different households. You might want to think about:

- how big a household is

- how often the activity takes place

- what they might be able to influence (for example, young people might be able to decide whether to have a bath or a shower, but they are less likely to be able to influence how their home is heated or cooled)

- how to record the evidence produced.

c) Now try out your questionnaire.

- See how it works with members of your class and what you learn from it.

- Summarise the data you gather in a clear and logical way.

Developing

There are several gases that contribute to the **greenhouse effect**. To compare different activities, scientists use the term carbon dioxide equivalent (CO_2e), which means that whichever **greenhouse gas** an activity releases, its effect is measured in terms of mass of carbon dioxide.

For example, it is estimated that a single cow has a CO_2e of 3.1 gigatons per year. This doesn't mean that the cow releases 3.1 gigatons of carbon dioxide annually, but the gases it does release (such as methane) have the same effect on the atmosphere as that equivalent amount of CO_2. The table shows some daily activities and their CO_2e.

Common daily activities and their carbon dioxide equivalent.

Activity	Carbon dioxide equivalent
Sending a text message	0.01 g
Using a disposable carrier bag	10 g
Boiling a litre of water using an electric kettle	70 g
Watching an hour's television on a 50-cm screen	88 g
Buying and drinking a 500-ml bottle of water	160 g
Driving 1.6 km in an average car	710 g
Using a litre of petrol	3150 g

Source: Mike Berners-Lee, *How Bad Are Bananas*, Profile Books, London. 2020

4 Look at the activities in the table above and see how they compare.

   a) Suggest why watching television affects the environment.

   b) Would tap water have the same CO_2e as bottled water? Why?

   c) Select another activity (not in the table above) and find out what its CO_2e figure is.

5 Research the CO_2e figures for different ways of doing the same activity. For example, you could compare the figures for walking a kilometre, cycling a kilometre and driving a kilometre.

   • Record the information – and also the sources you use.

   • Calculate how much CO_2e is saved by doing the activity one way rather than another.

Travelling 1.6 km by car	Walking 1.6 km	Cycling 1.6 km
0.44 kg CO_2e	0.02 kg CO_2e – saving 0.42 kg over driving	0.01kg CO_2e – saving 0.43 kg over driving

Final task

You should now be able to develop some clear guidance to people in your class about how to reduce their carbon footprint. You have:

- learned what a carbon footprint is

- used primary research (in your survey) to explore what might be affecting the size of a person's carbon footprint

- used secondary research to determine what difference changing aspects of your lives might make.

6 Working in a small group and using your primary and secondary research:

   a) Identify changes that people could make to reduce their carbon footprint

   b) Determine what impact this would have.

   - Think about a good way of displaying this information such as a poster or information leaflet.

   - Make it clear what a difference it would make if, for example, someone was to have a shower instead of a bath or to cut out meat from their diet.

   - Display your ideas alongside those from other groups. Between you, the class should be able to come up with a whole set of planet-saving ideas.

② REFLECTION POINT

In this unit, you have been learning about accessing information from various sources and presenting it in ways that are informative and persuasive. What advice would you give someone who was:

- designing questions to put to people to gather information and attitudes

- researching information on the internet

- presenting information for people to access and understand easily?

Applying what you have learned

Skills focus

✓ Research
✓ Evaluation

Learning focus

- Demonstrate how research can locate information that informs decision-making.
- Evaluate information and evidence gathered to suggest effective actions.

Your task

In this chapter, you have looked at several aspects of being more sustainable, including managing waste, being self-sufficient in energy and reducing carbon dioxide emissions. These can all make a positive contribution, but some may be easier than others to implement.

Your task, as a group, is to research, develop and promote a specific action for your school to consider adopting to make it more sustainable.

Approaching the task

1 First, identify a possible area of development for the school. You could use some of the ideas you have explored in this chapter, or you could use something different. For example:

- You could look at transport and the way that students and staff get to and from the school.

- You could look at energy and how the school is powered.

- You could use your research into the management of waste from earlier in the chapter.

This should lead you to decide about the aspect to focus on. Make it one specific idea to focus upon.

(2) Next, research what the school could actually do. Rather than just say, for example, that there should be solar panels on the roof, you could find out how much of the roof area has a favourable aspect (that is, faces in a suitable direction), what the area is and how much energy they could be expected to generate. This research will make your case more persuasive. If you were exploring the recycling of a particular material, you could find out what could be recycled in your area, how it could be gathered and what benefit it would make to your community.

(3) Finally, make a group presentation that would promote your action. Think about not only the change you want to see but also the audience. The way to persuade senior leaders may not be the same as the way to encourage students in the school.

Checklist for success

✔ Are you clear about the change you are making a case for? Anyone seeing your proposal should be in no doubt.

✔ Have you researched it carefully and thoroughly? The more supporting (and better) evidence you can gather, the more persuasive your case will be.

✔ Have you made the benefits clear? What will people gain from supporting your ideas?

✔ Have you designed the presentation for the audience you will be presenting to, thinking about what will interest and engage them?

Reflecting on your progress

Think back over this chapter.

- Pick out three examples of research you have done that were useful.

- Select one example of an activity where the point you were making was supported by relevant evidence you had found.

- Give an example of a good research question you posed and were then able to answer.

- Identify a key learning point for you from this chapter. What do you need to focus on to get even better at the skills of research?

What is your teacher looking for?

- You should be able to demonstrate that you can think clearly and logically. The problem, your solution and the evidence should fit together well.

- Your research should be clear and thorough. It should be of quality, easily checked and relevant. Sources should be referenced.

- You should be SMART about the change you are wanting to see. People should see what you are proposing and be likely to respond, 'I can do that – and it will make a difference'.

Check your progress

Beginning	Developing	Going beyond
• I can produce a question that can be researched and suggest how to answer it. • I can locate relevant information and present it. • I can suggest whether the information is relevant.	• I can develop and refine a question that can be researched and propose a clear strategy to gather evidence. • I can use a variety of sources and organise what I have found in a logical way. • I can begin to evaluate the relative value and relevance of the evidence gathered.	• I can construct and critique research questions and justify strategies for gathering evidence to answer them. • I can critically use a wide range of sources and organise findings effectively and logically. • I can critically evaluate the sources of the evidence presented.

Next steps

Look for opportunities to use the research skills you have developed in other parts of your education; these are transferable skills and applicable to a range of contexts.

Look at newspaper or magazine articles with the same critical eye that you have used in this chapter; you are likely to find that some of them stand up to scrutiny much better than others.

Learn the sources of information that seem to be particularly useful; these may be worth referring to in other activities. Bookmark these sources if they are online and share them with other students in your class. Reliable sources are valuable.

Exploring arguments
Development, trade and aid

Where communities are isolated or run down and struggling to support people financially, local people may look for ways to boost the economy. Development of a region is often achieved through trade and tourism – but what can be the cost of this?

In this chapter, you will be exploring the topic of 'Development, trade and aid', thinking about the following issues:

- **Why might people support or object to a development near where they live?**

- **Are National Parks a good way of developing an area sustainably?**

- **Should tourists be limited or even banned from visiting well-known beauty spots?**

- **Is tourism the best route to sustainable development?**

You will be developing a range of research, analysis and evaluation skills:

3.1 Identifying ideas from different perspectives

3.2 Explaining graphical and numerical data

3.3 Evaluating the credibility of sources

3.4 Evaluating the effectiveness of an argument

3.5 Applying what you have learned

Your final task will be to prepare for and participate in a debate arguing for or against a local development.

Identifying ideas from different perspectives

Skills focus
✓ Analysis
Learning focus
• Identify the different perspectives people have on an issue.
• Explain how people use evidence to support what they say.

Big question: Why might people support or object to a development near where they live?

Getting started

1 What would be your dream holiday? Would it be near a sun-kissed beach or a buzzing city centre? Or somewhere else?

Working with a partner, discuss where you would go, where you would stay and how you would get there.

Exploring

It is difficult to think of holiday destinations before they became popular. Hotels are an accepted part of towns and cities, and trips to see ancient or natural wonders are what most tourists expect. But is this sort of development a good thing?

2 Look at the photo and read the description that goes with it.

Illegal Hotel El Algarrobico demolition action in Spain

Greenpeace activists on the beach at El Algarrobico, 2016.

Greenpeace activists write 'demolition' on the beach of El Algarrobico. Exactly 10 years ago to the day, the construction of the **illegal** hotel was blocked. After a decade of campaigning, Greenpeace celebrates the decision of the Spanish Supreme Court to demolish the hotel El Algarrobico, officially declaring the site **rural** land.

Source: Greenpeace.

> ### Vocabulary
>
> **Greenpeace**: campaigning organisation that wants to protect the environment
>
> **activist**: someone who takes actions to bring about change
>
> **demolition**: destruction of a building
>
> **illegal**: against the law
>
> **rural**: relating to the countryside

When you read a source, it is important to understand the ideas in it and to identify what the **viewpoint** or **perspective** of the writer is. Asking some basic questions can help you in this process.

3 Discuss these questions with a partner:

a) Who has produced this text and photo? When was it produced? (Why might this matter?)

b) What is it about? What information do the text and photo reveal?

c) What opinions does it contain? Is this supported by any evidence?

d) Can you trust the information given? Why?

e) What do you think the perspective of the people or organisation who produced the source is? Why?

f) How – if at all – has the source helped you answer the big question 'Why might people support or object to a development near where they live'?

The photo and text present a clear message about development. However, it is only one side of the story.

Developing

Imagine there is a beautiful natural location near where you live (for example, a lake, stretch of coastline or forest). It is undeveloped, has few roads, and some, but not many, inhabitants. Your local or national government is considering making it into an attractive place for people to visit and stay.

Who might have a perspective on the development of the natural location? Here are some possibilities.

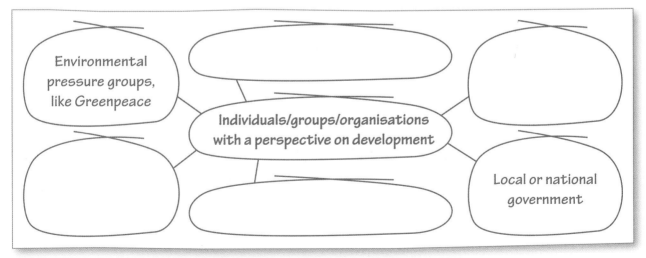

Environmental pressure groups, like Greenpeace

Individuals/groups/organisations with a perspective on development

Local or national government

4 Working with a partner, copy and complete the diagram, adding any further people or organisations that might have an interest in the development.

5 Who do you think might have made the statements below? Working with a partner, discuss each statement and link it to the perspectives in your diagram or any others you can think of.

A

> We need investment. Our roads are dreadful, and it would be great to have regular bus routes to out-of-reach places. This would win us many votes!

B

> Lots of forest will have to be cut down to make space for hotels. Wildlife will be destroyed.

C

> There is no work for me here. But if tourists come, I can take them on hunting or fishing trips nearby.

D

> I have lived here for 50 years. If outsiders come, it will change everything. Our children, and our children's children, will forget their roots and want to leave.

From this, you can see that a perspective is a viewpoint plus evidence. For example: 'I do/don't want development because…'

6 Now, read this interview. Then, working on your own, write answers to the questions below.

I believe development can be a good thing if it is sustainable. For example, as a local hotel-owner, I would like to see my hotel in this new resort, but I would insist on all hotels having a limit of three storeys. They would also have to be built from local, natural materials, which fit the environment. I need this development because I can build my business, open new hotels, and give much-needed employment to local people such as taxi-drivers who could bring people from the main town to the hotel.

Source: Interview with local radio station, 2022.

a) What is this person's perspective? Who are they – and why do they have an interest in the issue?

b) What is their viewpoint and what (if any) evidence do they provide to support it?

c) What counter-arguments could someone make against this perspective?

d) How close or far is this perspective from Greenpeace's perspective? Why?

Final task

At the end of this chapter, you will be presenting your ideas about how a community can develop an area sustainably. Here is a simple map of the location with a few geographical details. Your local council has proposed that the shaded lilac area be developed.

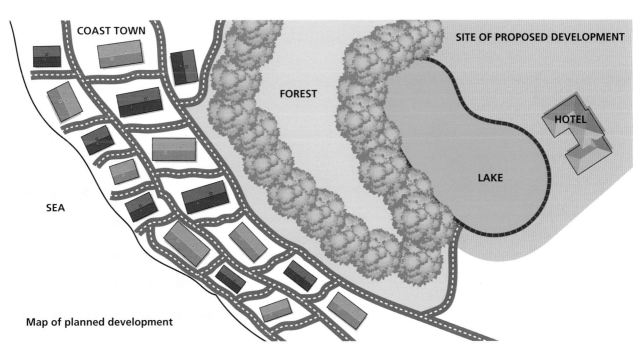

Map of planned development

7 **a)** In a small group, list at least six groups or individuals who would have a perspective on whether the development should be built.

b) Write down three potential advantages and three disadvantages to developing this area.

c) Note which of the groups you identified might use these points to support their perspective. Which might hold more than one perspective?

8 In the same group, allocate a role to each member (for example, hotel owner, parent of young children). Then have a short conversation arguing 'your' point of view on the development.

Language support

When identifying a perspective in a text, look for:

• verbs that convey emotion or beliefs (*believe, feel, think, love, hate*)

• positive/negative adjectives (*local, natural* materials; *much-needed* employment).

❓ REFLECTION POINT

• You have explored a small number of local perspectives on this issue. How easy or difficult did you find it to identify the key perspectives and viewpoints on the issue?

• What did you learn about the issue of development while doing this?

Explaining graphical and numerical data

Skills focus
✓ Analysis
Learning focus
- Identify the graphical or numerical data in a source.
- Explain how the graphical or numerical data support an argument or perspective.

Big question: Are national parks a good way of developing an area sustainably?

Getting started

Have you heard of 'National Parks'? They are generally large, natural spaces owned by the government that are preserved and protected in law. Often, they have a strong conservation goal and are intended to symbolise national pride. Four well-known ones are:

| Yellowstone | Serengeti | Shennongjia | Kaziranga |

1 Working in a group of four, choose one park each and quickly research it. Find out:

- where the park is
- at least one species it is famous for or is trying to preserve
- why people might visit it.

Exploring

People who wish to argue for or against a particular course of action often use **data** to support their argument. They do this for several reasons:

White Desert National Park, Egypt.

- Data is **quantifiable** and is often seen as pure fact as opposed to emotional **assertion**.
- Data can show **trends** or changes over time, enabling someone to make comparisons.
- Data can be carefully selected in order to stress the evidence in support of one view.
- Data can be presented in graphic ways that are memorable.

In the last unit, you began to think about developing a local natural area. One key question you might ask is: Can you preserve a natural area *and* develop it at the same time?

Look at the **infographic** created by the US National Park Service. The heading states 'National Parks benefit *you*' – which here probably means citizens of the USA.

> ### 🔑 Key terms
>
> **data**: facts and statistics (numerical data) gathered for analysis
>
> **quantifiable**: can be measured in a scientific way
>
> **assertion**: a statement presented as fact without supporting evidence
>
> **trend**: a general development in the way something happens
>
> **infographic**: information displayed in a visually interesting way

2 How does the National Park Service use data to support this perspective? Working with a partner, answer these questions:

a) Four large numbers are clearly visible. What do these refer to?

b) What other data measures can you find?

c) The infographic features fir trees, a bison or buffalo and a flying bird. What data are given about trees, animals or the landscape itself?

3 Three students have been discussing the infographic and its perspective – the 'message' or argument it conveys. Working on your own, write brief answers to these questions:

a) What are the different conclusions each student has drawn from the infographic?

b) Which of the students (if any) do you think is right about the perspective?

Source: National Park Service, US Department of the Interior, 2020.

Student A:	Well, the pictures of animals make it clear the argument is all about how they're preserving nature.
Student B:	Really? There are no statistics or data on conservation.
Student A:	Isn't that obvious though? The whole point is to preserve nature.
Student C:	Then, why not mention that? Everything the infographic shows is about money. How it's good value for the US **taxpayer** – brings in cash.
Student B:	Hmm. It does mention visitor numbers, so they're also arguing that the popularity of the parks makes it all worthwhile.
Student C:	Yeah – but only in terms of what visitors spend and how it creates loads of jobs.

4 Write a sentence summing up the perspective of the National Park Service, including its argument and reasons. You could start:

The Parks Service argues that…

> **Vocabulary**
>
> **taxpayer**: someone who pays a proportion of what they earn to the government

Developing

Simple figures such as the ones in the infographic are often used to support an argument. The same is sometimes done using graphs or tables. However, data of any sort need to be analysed as carefully as any other evidence. For example:

- Is the sample taken large enough to draw conclusions?

- Is the time, date or period when it was taken significant in any way?

- Does the sample include all the relevant data or is anything missed out (consciously or accidentally)?

- Does the sample show any trends?

These useful pointers can be added to the questions you answered in Unit 3.1 about who produced the source, why it was produced, the credibility of the author/publisher and so on.

5 Read this press release from the environmental team that works for a local government responsible for putting 'protected status' on a local beauty spot to stop it being developed. Then discuss the questions below in a small group.

Our annual report is strong evidence that giving Vergreen Woods (an area of 4 square kilometres) protected status in 2017 has been worth it. We have seen substantial benefits, especially in **biodiversity**.

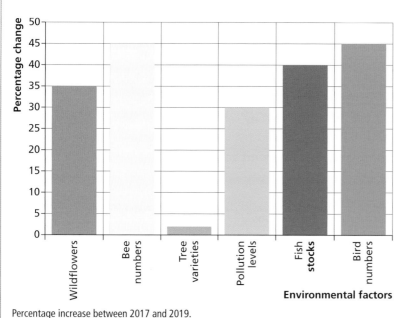

Percentage increase between 2017 and 2019.

> **Vocabulary**
>
> **biodiversity**: varieties of species in one area
>
> **stocks**: supply or quantity
>
> **flawed**: based on errors or lacking something

a) What is the argument being made here?

b) Who is making the argument – and why? Are they **credible**?

c) Is the period for the survey credible?

d) Do the figures given support the argument about biodiversity? Why?

e) Is the **data set** sufficiently detailed?

f) Is anything missing from the data?

🔑 Key terms

credible: believable

data set: collection of linked data (information)

Final task

6 Working on your own, write 100–150 words comparing the arguments and the evidence used to support both sources. Use this structure to help you.

> The infographic produced by the National Parks Service argues that…
>
> This is supported by…
>
> However, the argument could be questioned because…

> The bar chart produced by the environmental team argues the case that…
>
> This is supported by…
>
> However, the argument could be questioned because…

❓ REFLECTION POINT

Have you ever thought how facts or numbers could be used to support arguments and whether these were trustworthy? Understanding how they are used is a good life skill as well as being useful in school or college work.

* Find examples of data or statistics used in the media or other sources you read.

* Why have these numbers been used?

* Are they persuasive – or do you think they are **flawed**? If so, how?

Language support

When you are analysing any argument supported by data or statistics, use these helpful words and phrases to summarise the findings:

* increase, rise, growth, surge

* decrease, drop, fall, reduction, decline, loss

* majority, high proportion of, greater, larger, numerous

* minority, low proportion of, lesser, smaller, few, rare.

Evaluating the credibility of sources

Skills focus
✓ Evaluation

Learning focus
- Identify the author and purpose in a source.
- Evaluate how credible a source is.

Big question: Should tourists be limited or even banned from visiting well-known beauty spots?

Getting started

Before 2010, a few thousand visitors each year visited a beauty spot called Horseshoe Bend near a small town called Page in Arizona, USA. By 2018, it was estimated that 2 million were visiting this isolated place.

Sightseers at Horseshoe Bend, Arizona.

1 Why do you think this happened? How do you think local people reacted?

Exploring

2 Now read the extract on page 47 from a travel blog on a holiday agency website.

When you read a source such as this, you are trying to establish three main things:

1. What am I being told?

2. Does this source help me answer the question I am researching (is it relevant)?

3. If so, can I trust what the writer/author tells me?

Now, work through each question in turn, writing your own answers down.

3 What are you being told?

a) Who is the writer? What are they describing or writing about?

b) What information do they give?

c) What is the purpose of the article they have written?

d) What is their viewpoint or perspective on the issue? (This may be the same as the purpose of the article.)

e) What information or evidence (if any) do they provide?

f) What else might tell us their perspective? For example, do they use **emotive** words or phrases?

> 🔑 **Key terms**
>
> **emotive**: showing strong feelings (for example, 'I *love* tourist spots')

How we are destroying one of the most scenic places in India: Ladakh

by Sinchita Mitra, student blogger, 31 August, 2019

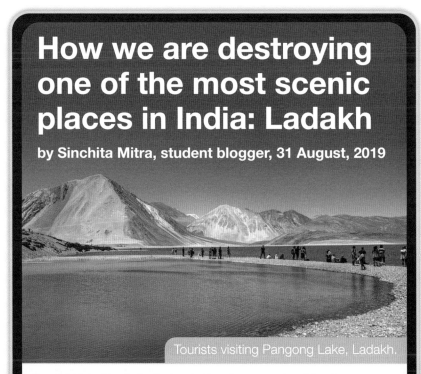

Tourists visiting Pangong Lake, Ladakh.

[Ladakh] in North India had often been praised for its amazing beauty, yet a long time ago not many Indians travelled here. It was a place out of limits, and too distant to travel to. But, that one scene from the superhit **Bollywood** movie ['3 Idiots'] seemed to change everything. If Ladakh knew what was going to happen, as **Aamir Khan** reunited with his college mates at its picturesque blue lake, it would have strongly opposed the idea of any movie being shot there. After the movie, Indian tourists started heading over to this exceedingly beautiful lake and flocking to it in **hordes**.

It was estimated that before this film was released, around 400,000 Indians visited Ladakh – but after the release of the film, the figures doubled and have still been growing at an **exponential rate**.

The Pangong Lake – which became the hub of tourists – was once untouched by humanity, yet today it is **cluttered** with cafés, washrooms, and **props** from the movies. All this is done to further boost tourism in the city. What this has led to is a staggering effect on both the environment and on the lives of the locals.

The once crystal-clear waters of canals in **Leh** are now filled with plastic water bottles that were casually thrown there. There are now traffic jams in a place where cars were a rarity once. Due to the upsurge of these cars **plying** for the tourists, the air now has an acute pollution issue. It is no more the kind of air that can cleanse your soul.

Source: Memorable India.

Vocabulary

Bollywood: Indian film studios nicknamed 'Bollywood'

Aamir Khan: Indian film actor

hordes: huge numbers

exponential rate: increasing more and more quickly

cluttered: untidily filled up with

props: items used in a play or film

Leh: largest city in Ladakh

plying: supplying or selling (here, trips to tourist destinations)

4 How relevant is the source to the big question you are researching?: 'Should tourists be limited or even banned from visiting well-known beauty spots?'

Find examples in each case to support your answer and share them with a partner.

a) Is the text about tourists?

b) Does it describe or talk about a 'well-known beauty spot'?

c) The question uses the word 'should' which requires you to give your view. So, is the text one that gives a view on this issue?

Developing

The first two questions lead you to the more complex third question: Can I trust what I am being told? Is the source credible?

It is important to understand that whether a source is credible is not the same as asking whether you agree with the argument it makes. For example, a well-respected Antarctic scientist might argue in *New Scientist* magazine that melting ice is not a result of climate change.

• They are *credible* because of their expertise and background and because the source is a respected science journal.

• However, you – or other scientists – may have a *different perspective* altogether, supported by a competing argument and evidence.

Ice melting in Antarctica.

5 Discuss the answer to this third question – about the source's credibility – with a partner.

a) What is the writer's role or position? Do they have a particular expertise from what you can tell? Do they have the 'ability to see' (that is, is the writer in a position to make a judgement about the issue)?

b) What evidence for their views do they give? Is this primary evidence (something they have direct experience of) or secondary – or both?

c) Do they – or the website/organisation – have a vested interest in telling you this? (You could consider whether the fact this is a holiday travel company is important.)

Leh, the largest city in Ladakh.

Final task

6 Imagine you have been given the task of deciding what to do about increased tourist numbers in Ladakh. Several options are possible:

- Do nothing: the popularity of the lake must have some positives.

- Give guidance or set rules about how visitors should behave.

- Ban or limit visitors altogether.

- Do something else of your choosing.

Working in a small group, decide what would be the best option and create a joint statement of 125–150 words summarising your viewpoint and reasons.

You may need to do some further research into the situation in Ladakh or look at what other places have done in response to higher visitor numbers (for example, at Horseshoe Bend).

? REFLECTION POINT

The text on page 47 is only a small part of a longer blog. In the later sections, the writer gives a range of guidance to tourists visiting popular locations. Here is one example:

> Embrace the true culture of Ladakh. Due to the influx of tourists, Ladakh has now become filled with English cafés and American food chains. All these places are only filling the pockets of the multinational companies. Head over to an authentic local restaurant and help the locals.

Source: Memorable India.

What is the writer's perspective here? Is there an alternative view that could be argued? If so, what is it?

Evaluating the effectiveness of an argument

Skills focus
✓ Evaluation
Learning focus
- Identify the structure and evidence used in an argument.
- Discuss how effective the argument is, referring to structure and evidence.

Big question: Is tourism the best route to sustainable development?

Getting started

In previous units, you explored how tourism can have damaging impacts on communities as well as bringing in money to local businesses. But does development have to be about tourism?

SIDS is the **acronym** for 'Small Island Developing States' and refers to (mostly) isolated islands such as Samoa (shown in the picture) that struggle economically for a range of reasons.

Apia, the capital city of Samoa.

Some of the problems SIDS face are:

- vulnerability to climate events

- small population size

- remoteness from international markets

- poor transport links

- fragile land and sea **ecosystems**.

1 Work with a partner to discuss why these might be problems, thinking of examples (for example, 'vulnerability to climate events' could mean when there are huge storms, these can devastate islands which are difficult to protect).

> **Vocabulary**
>
> **acronym**: word formed from the first letter of key words in a phrase or title
>
> **ecosystem**: organisms living and interacting within a particular physical environment
>
> **stop-over**: a place where a long journey is broken (usually for at least one night)

Exploring

When we read sources that contain arguments, like the ones in Units 3.2 and 3.3, we make judgements about how convincing those arguments are. This can include evaluating the following factors:

- The writer or organisation's own experience and feelings, and how relevant they are

- Their 'ability to see' – this links to the above but means whether they can judge or not; for example, someone might have strong views on city traffic but live in the countryside, which might weaken their position to judge

- The extent to which they use evidence-based points rather than assertions (statements with no evidence)

- Other forms of evidence they use to support a point – this could include facts, data, what other people say, the results of surveys or other primary research

- How varied the evidence is – are they drawing on just one example or more?

- How logical or well-structured their argument is – for example, does it make a clear link between cause and effect? If someone says 'City traffic has tripled since they opened the new coast road', then a link between the two has been made. Does the writer make parts of their argument clear by using subheadings or different paragraphs for different points?

2 Sentences a–c are from someone arguing for the opening of a new airport on an island. Read the arguments, then note down how each sentence matches one or more of the factors above.

a
'As a local taxi-driver, I noticed how new businesses began to open even before the first bit of concrete was laid.'

b
'The new airport is halfway between the two continents, which might mean it becomes a popular **stop-over** for tourists, like Dubai or Hong Kong.'

c
'When a similar airport on the next island opened, there was an immediate surge in visitors who spent more than 50 million dollars locally.'

3 Working with a partner, take turns to argue one of the following points using your own experience as evidence.

I would like to see more/ fewer tourists in my local area because…	Our school should make more links with schools in other areas because…	I wish we had the chance to buy more/fewer products from around the world because…

Developing

4 Read this article, in which a resident of Bali explains why they believe tourism is *not* the only solution to developing their area. Consider:

- How do they make their argument?

- How convincing is it?

I used to work in a shop selling beachwear to tourists, but during the Covid pandemic the tourists stayed away and I lost my job. Normally, we had around six million international visitors a year, but in the first ten months of 2020, Bali had just 45 tourists (according to an article on the **Al Jazeera** website)! So, I had no choice but to find another career.

I started selling **organic** fruit and veg boxes from produce grown in my aunt's garden (which she rents out to me). I only sell to local people, so I keep my prices low – but the money is going to me, not the shopkeeper, and if the weather stays fine, it is more reliable work than the tourists.

Lots of young people I know now want to be **entrepreneurs** running their own businesses. One wants to develop a freshwater **eel farm** – as everyone knows the Balinese love eel crackers. Another has set up a bike repair shop as people are avoiding cars because of energy costs. All these things are about serving our community, not tourists.

5 **a)** Working on your own, copy and complete the table below, making a judgement about each element of the argument.

For column 3, decide how convincing the argument is and score it from 1–5, where 1 is least convincing and 5 is most convincing. Then give your reasons for your decision in column 4.

Feature	Examples from text	How convincing (1–5)	Why/why not
Writer's own experience and/or 'ability to see'			
Makes evidence-based points			
Uses data/statistics to support points			
Varies types of evidence used			
Argument is well organised and structured			
Links points well (for example, using connectives)			
Any other strengths or weaknesses			

b) Share your completed table with a partner and update it once you have agreed responses.

c) Then, think about any potential flaws (over and above those you already identified).

Final task

6 Based on your completed table, write at least two paragraphs on how convincing the article is. You could use these prompts:

I think that in general, the writer makes a convincing/ unconvincing argument because firstly, they…

In addition, they state that…which shows…

7 When you have finished, add your paragraph to a class display. Read through the other paragraphs and note down what was done well and any areas for improvement. Share your findings as a whole class.

❓ REFLECTION POINT

How easy would it be to replace tourism in places you know locally or in your country? What sorts of trade or employment could fill the gap – if any? Would you miss out on other things (not necessarily money) if tourists stayed away?

Make a list of points arguing for or against increased tourism in your local area or country.

Language support
. . . .

When you comment on another person's argument, you will sometimes need to quote their words directly. For example:

The writer argues that 'the weather is more reliable' than tourists.

Note how the quoted words go inside speech or quotation marks.

Applying what you have learned

Skills focus
✓ Evaluation
✓ Communication

Learning focus
- Present arguments, supporting them with evidence.
- Listen and respond to what others say and show you understand the issues.

Your task

Developers are planning to build a hotel and leisure complex in an isolated but beautiful location near your town. There is to be a **public meeting** chaired by your teacher to decide whether to go ahead with the development. You will play a role arguing for or against the following statement:

'We believe that the Lakeside Development will have a positive impact on the local community.'

Vocabulary

public meeting: an open meeting at which local people give their views on an issue concerning them

Approaching the task

Look again at the site plan from Unit 3.1. The shaded area is the designated area for the development.

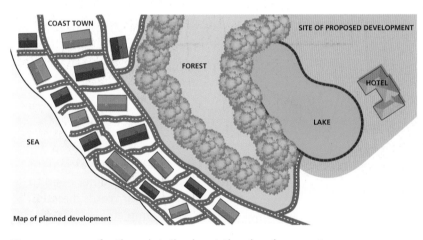

Map of planned development

Here are some further details about the development:

- The hotel will provide 50 jobs for local workers.

- The lake contains one protected fish species.

- The lake is currently used for family days out, picnics and swimming. There is free parking.

- Traffic will increase by about 25 per cent across the town and region. There will be new bus routes.

- No new schools or medical facilities are planned.

1 a) Note down reasons for and against the development. Then share these in a small group.

b) Your teacher will allocate you one of these roles:

- Owner of hotel and leisure chain (from outside area)
- Local businessperson (for example, shop owners)
- Local schoolteacher
- Local farmer or farmworker

- Fisherman/woman
- Taxi-driver
- Young, unemployed person
- Environmental campaigner
- Parent/carer of child(ren) who live near lake.

2 Once you have been given a role, create a role-card that provides the following details:

- Your name, age and role
- Your perspective on the development (for/against)
- *At least two* pieces of supporting evidence (such as a statistic, a personal experience, a quotation from a report). The evidence can be taken from sources in this chapter or from your own research. You can make up some information yourself.

3 Take part in the public meeting in role. Speak and give your views, demonstrating your speaking and listening skills as well as presenting good arguments.

Read through the 'Checklist for success' for advice on giving a successful presentation.

Checklist for success

✔ Speak clearly and include the key points you wish to make.

✔ Vary the **tone** and **pitch** of your voice to stress key points.

✔ Listen carefully – you may want to **refute** what someone says.

✔ Do not interrupt or shout out: show respect to whoever is speaking, even if you disagree.

> **Reflecting on your progress**

After the public meeting has ended, reflect on your experience and make notes on the following:

- What were the key arguments?
- Who was most/least convincing? Why?
- What was the overall outcome or decision (if there was one)?
- How did you perform personally? Did you make your points convincingly?
- Regarding the development of isolated places, what is your perspective now? In what ways has it changed, if at all, from the beginning of the chapter?

🔑 Key terms

tone: the sound of your voice, which conveys your feelings, for example angry, uncertain

pitch: how high or low the sound of your voice is

refute: argue against

Language support

When presenting an argument, it is helpful to stress your idea and use causal connectives to support it.

Introductory phrases such as 'I strongly believe that…' or 'My main argument is that…' can be followed by:

- links such as 'because', 'so', 'in order that' within the same sentence
- phrases such as 'As a result of…', 'As a consequence of…', 'Due to…' at the start of subsequent sentences.

Check your progress

Beginning	Developing	Going beyond
• I can understand the main points in a source. • I can explain what basic data measures show. • I can identify the author and the main purpose of a source. • I can identify the main argument in a source. • I can give my view about an issue in a debate situation.	• I can comment on different perspectives on an issue in different sources. • I can explain how graphical and numerical data supports an argument. • I can comment on a range of elements from a source such as author, purpose, perspective and evidence. • I can explain the structure and evidence used in a source. • I can present an argument supporting it with evidence.	• I can compare the ideas and evidence from two different perspectives on an issue. • I can analyse how graphical and numerical data can be convincing and flawed. • I can evaluate a range of factors in a source to judge how credible it is. • I can comment on the effectiveness of an argument, referring to a range of factors. • I can demonstrate persuasive skills, presenting an argument logically.

Next steps

Research the effect of visitor numbers on a range of well-known locations, for example how the numbers climbing Everest have affected the landscape and environment. You could also do some historical research sourcing images that show how a specific place has grown and developed over time.

You could write your own set of tourist rules for anyone visiting a site of special interest. Think about what you could comment on, for example shopping, travel, respect, litter, noise, and so on.

Making interpretations

Migration

A migrant is someone who moves away from where they usually live. Their migration can be to somewhere else within a country: for example, from a village in the countryside to a city. Their migration can be to another country: international migration. Migration can be temporary. That means migrants move somewhere else for a time and then return to where they usually live. Or it can be permanent: people move away for the rest of their lives. There are also different reasons for migration.

In this chapter, you will be exploring the topic 'Migration and urbanisation', thinking about the following issues:

- **Why do people migrate?**
- **Should healthcare workers stay in the Philippines?**

- **What makes some sources about migration more credible than others?**
- **What makes some arguments about migration more effective than others?**

You will be developing a range of analysis and evaluation skills:

4.1 Identifying ideas and evidence from perspectives about migration

4.2 How is information used to support perspectives about migration?

4.3 Evaluating sources on migration

4.4 Effective arguments about migration

4.5 Applying what you have learned

Your final task will be to prepare for and carry out a class debate on the advantages and disadvantages of migration.

Identifying ideas and evidence from perspectives about migration

Skills focus
✓ Analysis

Learning focus
- Identify some different perspectives about migration.
- Identify ideas and select evidence for perspectives about migration.

Big question: Why do people migrate?

Getting started

Migration is when people move to live in a new area or country.

1 Why do you think people might choose to migrate? Working with a partner:

a) List all the reasons you can think of for internal migration – that is, moving to live elsewhere in the same country.

b) Now list all the reasons you can think of for external migration – moving to live in a different country.

c) What was the same for your lists? What was different?

Exploring

Here are two reflections on migration by people who have left their own countries. Read them and then answer the questions that follow.

Yerima, migrated from Togo to Spain

I lived with my parents until I was 18 years old. I worked as a driver but earned very little. So, I decided to leave for Europe. I went to Dakar where I spent six months, then to Mauritania. From there, I entered Europe via the Mediterranean.

A man is supposed to eat three times a day. If you have a family, you have to ensure they have food, shelter, medicine, and education. If you cannot provide those basic necessities for your family because of lack of opportunities in your country, then you have to try and find a way somewhere else.

I have a young daughter. When I left Togo, my daughter was just 2 months old. People may ask what kind of father I am, to leave behind my wife and infant daughter. But what kind of a father would I be, if I stayed and couldn't provide them a decent life?

So, you abandon everything you've ever known, and come to a foreign land, only to be subjected to all types of **discrimination** and **violations**. The very rights that international organisations are meant to protect. But there is nothing you can do about it, because you're not in your own land.

Source: Joe McCarthy – Global Citizen.

Shafaq, migrated from Syria to Lebanon

I used to have a peaceful life and live in my amazing home in Dera'a. I enjoyed the nature around my house and the food coming from the land. I woke up every morning to the sound of birds singing. The brutality of the **civil war** forced my family to leave this house and to start the journey to be **refugees**.

Since the start of our journey, we moved a lot in Lebanon, and I attended different schools. In the end, my family decided to go close to the border with Syria. We came to this area because just we want to survive. My father is working as an electrician and this is the only income for our family. All of my family we are living in a tiny house with one bedroom, a small kitchen, and a bathroom. We are considered illegal because we don't have official documents.

I am behind two years in school because of moving from one school to another. I am still doing very good in my school, and I will continue to do that. I want to finish my education to help my family, and to help other people who want to learn. I consider myself lucky to have Al Jalil Center. I got a lot of educational, emotional, and psychological support. I am also really sad because of the unknown future waiting for me. Every day I wonder where I will be tomorrow. Yes, it's an unknown future.

Source: Global Giving.

 2

a) What reasons does Yerima give for his migration?

b) What reason does Shafaq give for her migration?

c) Return to your list of reasons for external migration from the 'Getting started' activity. Did you include the reasons Yerima and Shafaq have given?

d) What has Yerima found difficult about his migration to Spain?

e) What has Shafaq found difficult about her migration to Lebanon?

f) What **perspectives** do you think Yerima and Shafaq have on their future?

> ### 🔑 Key term
>
> **perspective**: a viewpoint on an issue based on evidence and reasoning

> ### Vocabulary
>
> **migration**: the movement of people from one place to another to live there, either for a while or permanently
>
> **discrimination**: treating people unfairly because they appear different
>
> **violation**: acting in a way that breaks rules, such as international laws
>
> **civil war**: a war between citizens of the same country
>
> **refugee**: someone who is forced to migrate in order to escape war or other kinds of dangers

Developing

3 Read migration facts A–H below, then write definitions of the
following words (in green bold). You can use a dictionary to help you:

a) international migrants   b) Oceania

c) internal migrants   d) migrant workers

e) remittances   f) countries of origin

g) sources of remittances   h) international students

i) forcibly displaced people   j) refugees.

A. There were an estimated 281 million international migrants as of mid-year in 2020. That means
one in every 30 people in the world – 3.6 per cent of the world's population – is an international
migrant. 48 per cent were female and 52 per cent were male (UN DESA, 2020).

B. At mid-year 2020, around 31 per cent of international migrant populations were residing in Asia, 31 per
cent in Europe, 26 per cent in the Americas, 9 per cent in Africa and 3 per cent in Oceania (UN DESA, 2020).

C. There are many more internal migrants than international
migrants: 740 million people in 2009 (UNDP, 2009).

D. There were 169 million migrant workers in the world in
2019. Of these, 99 million were male migrant workers and 70
million were female migrant workers (ILO, 2021).

E. In 2021, migrants sent an estimated US$773 billion in remittances
to families and communities in their countries of origin. The top three
countries that received remittances in 2021 were India ($89 billion),
China ($53 billion) and Mexico (US$ 54 billion). The top three sources of
remittances were the USA, Saudi Arabia and China (Ratha et al., 2022).

F. In 2020, there were nearly 6.4 million international students globally (UNESCO, 2022).

G. There were 89.3 million forcibly displaced people around the world
at the end of 2021, around 40 per cent of whom were displaced across
international borders and 60 per cent within countries. Of these, 27.1
million were refugees (UNHCR, 2022).

Sources: Global Migration
Indicators 2021: Insights
from the Global Migration
Data Portal. International
Organization for Migration
(IOM), Geneva. Copyright ©
IOM GMDAC.; International
Organization for Immigration
(IOM); United Nations (UN);
UNESCO; International Labour
Organization (ILO).

H. There were 4.6 million asylum seekers globally at the end of 2021
(UNHCR, 2022). Asylum seekers are people who have left their country
and are waiting to see if another country will give them legal protection
as a refugee because of the dangers they face in their own country.

4 Read the following perspectives about migration.

For each one, match it to one or more of the migration facts on the opposite page. You are looking for a migration fact that either supports or argues against the perspective – some of the perspectives are misunderstandings about migration.

Vocabulary

asylum: a safe place or country to live in for people at risk from dangers in their own country

a)
> The movement of workers from lower-income origin countries to higher-income destination countries makes the migrant workers richer, makes the destination countries richer, and helps origin countries too because of the money that migrant workers send home.

> Most international migrants are asylum seekers, which means people who are fleeing their country because of war and who want to live in another country where they can be safer.

b)

c)
> Migrants are typically men, and most come from low-income countries and move to the USA and Europe.

Final task

5 Working on your own or in a small group, write an article for the school magazine or website on the reasons why people migrate.

- You could draw on facts in this unit and from your own research.

- You could support your chosen facts with real-life stories of migration (these could describe experiences you have had, or the experiences of people you know, or be from your own research).

- Aim to include information about migration in different countries and globally – don't focus on just one country.

- Your article could identify 'common myths of migration' and explain why they are not true.

- Aim to use some of the words linked to migration you have learned in this unit.

❓ REFLECTION POINT

Has there been migration in your family history? Remember that migration includes both internal and international movement.

Reflect on the opportunities and challenges of migration. Has your understanding of migration changed because of the work you have done in this unit? If so, how?

How is information used to support perspectives about migration?

Skills focus

✓ Analysis

Learning focus

• Find patterns in data.

• Explain how information is used to support a perspective.

Big question: Should healthcare workers stay in the Philippines?

Getting started

The Philippines is famous around the world for its healthcare workers (HCWs): 550 000 Filipinos are currently working in healthcare in other countries.

1 Read the extract from an online article about Filipino healthcare workers.

a) What impression of Filipino healthcare workers do you get from the article?

b) Do you think it's a good thing that many Filipino healthcare workers work abroad? Why/why not?

c) What problems might this type of migration create for the people living in the Philippines?

> **Vocabulary**
>
> **commending**: celebrating
>
> **lauded**: praised

If there's anything worth **commending** during the Covid-19 pandemic, it's the heroism and selflessness of the Filipino healthcare workers in the country and abroad who are risking their own lives to keep Covid-19 cases from getting out of control.

At the height of the pandemic, countries like the United Kingdom **lauded** around 21,000 Filipino frontliners who were working for the country's National Health Service and private hospitals for their extraordinary contribution to UK's battle against COVID-19.

However, long before the pandemic, Filipino healthcare workers have been in high demand abroad, with the Philippines being the highest exporters of healthcare workers in the world, particularly in nursing.

Source: 'Why are Filipino healthcare workers in high demand abroad?', *Manila Bulletin*, 6 September 2021.

Exploring

2 Study the sources of information below.

a) What does Source A tell you about the number of Filipino healthcare workers (HCWs) working overseas?

b) For each of Sources B–E, say what information you take from it about Filipinos migrating to work as HCWs. Record your findings in a table.

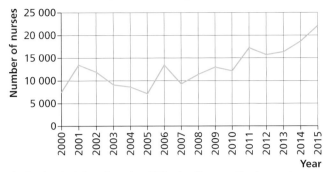

Source A: Filipino nurses working overseas between 2000 and 2015.

Author's calculations based on Philippine Overseas Employment agency.

Y. Y. Ortiga (2018) 'Learning to fill the labor niche: Filipino nursing graduates and the risk of the migration trap', *The Russell Sage Foundation Journal of the Social Sciences.* (c) 2018 Russell Sage Foundation https://www.rsfjournal.org/content/4/1/172

Source B: The countries of origin of high-skilled migrants living in **OECD** countries.

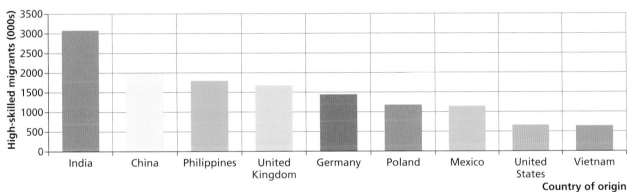

Source: OECD.

Source C: Filipino nurses being trained at the start of the 20th century. The Philippines had been a Spanish **colony**, but the USA took control of it in 1898. Filipinos were taught English and learned about American culture. Many women were **recruited** to be nurses. Some of them went to the USA to study nursing; some stayed, and others returned home.

Vocabulary

OECD: Organisation for Economic Co-operation and Development. Most of its 38 member countries are high-income countries with democratic governments, such as the USA, Germany, the UK and Sweden.

colony: a country controlled by a more powerful country

recruited: hired

Source D: Data comparing average monthly salaries for registered nurses in four countries compared to the Philippines.

Country	Average monthly salary for a registered nurse (2020), in US dollars
Philippines	604
USA	6985
Saudi Arabia	3316
Japan	3054
United Kingdom	2489

Source E: Countries with migrant populations of between 10 000 and 1 million+ Filipinos in 2017. In 2021, the Philippines had a total population of 109 million.

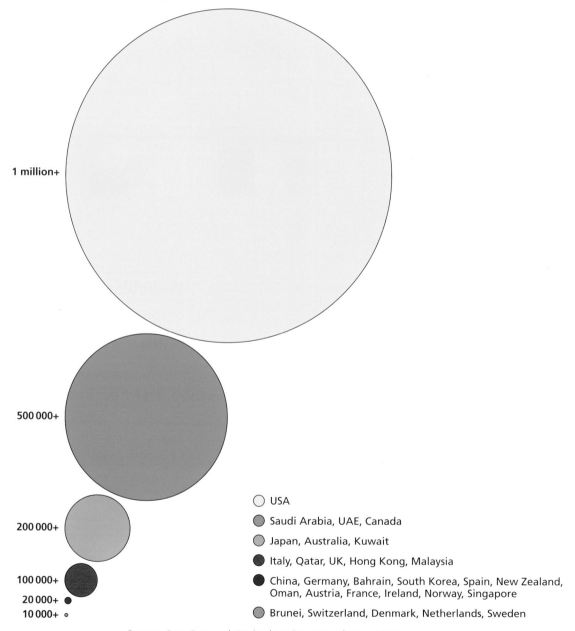

1 million+

500 000+

200 000+

100 000+

20 000+

10 000+

○ USA
● Saudi Arabia, UAE, Canada
● Japan, Australia, Kuwait
● Italy, Qatar, UK, Hong Kong, Malaysia
● China, Germany, Bahrain, South Korea, Spain, New Zealand, Oman, Austria, France, Ireland, Norway, Singapore
● Brunei, Switzerland, Denmark, Netherlands, Sweden

Source: Pew Research/United Nations Population Division.

3 Use the information you have gathered from Sources A–E to write your own perspective with this heading: 'Why I think many healthcare workers from the Philippines work in higher-income countries'.

> Remember: a perspective needs to include evidence or reasoning.

Developing

In March 2020, the government stopped Filipino HCWs from leaving the Philippines to work in other countries. The Philippines needed all its medical workers because of the Covid-19 pandemic.

The ban ended in November 2020. However, the government still put a limit on how many HCWs could work abroad. In November 2020, it said 5000 HCWs could leave the Philippines.

4 Each of the speech bubbles on this page represents an argument about the government's decision to ban or reduce HCW migration.

  a) Identify the arguments that are being made. Put them in your own words.

  b) Identify where **factual evidence** is used to support the arguments.

  c) Which statements use **anecdotal evidence** to support their arguments?

  d) Are any of these statements an assertion?

🔑 Key terms

factual evidence: evidence based on facts; data that can be shown to be true

anecdotal evidence: evidence based on people's own experiences

A: I am a minister in the government of the Philippines. Last year, 19 000 HCWs left our country to work in other countries. That cannot continue this year. We need to make sure we have enough medical professionals to fight the pandemic here in the Philippines.

B: If the government wants us to stay working in healthcare in the Philippines, then we need higher wages and better working conditions. We have the lowest HCW salaries in southeast Asia.

C: We rely on the money my son Mark earns as a nurse in the USA. Without the money he sends home, we couldn't afford our electricity bill or even to buy enough food for us all.

D: My sister works in a hospital in London. In 2020, far more Asian nurses died of Covid there than White healthcare workers. They put the Asian nurses on the front line, taking all the risks. Asian nurses are not treated well in these countries.

E: I work as a manager at a city hospital in California, USA. We have often relied on Filipino nurses, who are highly skilled. In 2020, we had to ask each nurse to care for more patients. That was dangerous for patients and for nurses.

Final task

5 **a)** What is your view on the Philippines' decision to stop any HCWs leaving to work abroad during the early months of the pandemic – from March to November 2020 – and then to limit how many could work abroad after that? Was it right or wrong? Discuss your reasons with a partner.

b) If you were the health minister of the Philippines in November 2020, how would you decide how many permits to give out each year so that HCWs could leave to work abroad? Use the data in this unit, including Sources F–H below, to help you make your decision. Then write a statement of no more than 150 words, to the Philippines government explaining your decision. Make sure you refer to the evidence you have used to support your decision.

Source F: Remittances sent from the rest of the world to the Philippines, 2016–2020

Year	Remittances to the Philippines, in US dollars
2016	31.14 billion
2017	32.81 billion
2018	33.81 billion
2019	35.17 billion
2020	34.88 billion

Source: World Bank.

Source G: Key medical information for 2020. (Healthcare statistics are often measured per 10 000 population, which means how many nurses or doctors there are for every 10 000 people in a region.)

	Number of nurses per 10000 population	Number of hospital beds per 10000 population	Severe Covid-19 cases as a percentage of hospital beds
National Capital Region	12	13.5	247
Philippines as a whole	8.2	6.1	93
USA (for comparison)	11.7	20.8	

Source: University of the Philippines Covid-19 Pandemic Response Team.

Source H: Numbers of new Covid-19 cases in the Philippines in 2020.

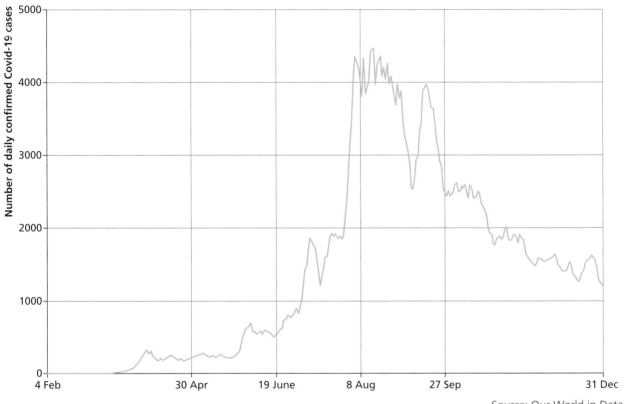

Source: Our World in Data.

> **❓ REFLECTION POINT**
>
> Have any sources you looked at in this unit changed your views on migration? If so, how have your views changed? For example, are there benefits or problems linked to migration that you weren't aware of before?
>
> If you were a healthcare worker in your country, what factors might encourage you to move abroad to work in another country? What factors might make you choose to stay in your home country?

How is information used to support perspectives about migration?

Evaluating sources on migration

Skills focus
✓ Evaluation
Learning focus
- Discuss the strengths and limitations of a source.
- Consider what makes some sources more credible than others.

Big question: What makes some sources about migration more credible than others?

Getting started

1 Your friend has moved to a new apartment, in a new part of your city. You have their address but you're not sure how to get there. You have a map app, a photo of the new apartment, and your neighbour has lived in the city for many years.

a) For each of these three sources of information, say one way in which they *could* be **useful** in finding your friend's new apartment.

b) Which of these three sources of information would you **trust** most to get you to your friend's new home?

c) Explain why you think this source of information would be more **reliable** than the other two.

Exploring

You already know from Stage 7 that sources can have strengths and limitations, for example:

- relevance – is a source relevant to your research question or not?

- bias – if a source unfairly ignores evidence against its perspective or is prejudiced, it is biased. Biased sources can still be useful, but a biased source is less reliable.

You also need to consider who the author of the source is. Authors in a position to know about the question you are researching should provide stronger sources than authors who are not.

> **🔑 Key terms**
>
> **useful**: something we can use for some purpose
>
> **trust**: a belief in someone or something
>
> **reliable**: dependable, trustworthy

2 Below are four sources from people commenting on government plans to increase the number of international students studying in a country.

    a) If the question is 'Why does the government want to increase the number of international students in the country?', which of the four people are in the best position to know?

    b) If the question is 'What should be done to make international students feel welcome at universities in this country?', then who is in the best position to know?

A: The head of a university, appearing on a TV report about the new plans

> We are always very happy to welcome more international students to our amazing university. Our courses are excellent, and we have plenty of support to help students feel welcome here.

B: A government official who is working on the new plans, making a speech to business leaders

> We value the skills and talents that international students bring with them, both during their period of study and afterwards if they choose to stay and work in this country.

C: An international student at university in the country, emailing a friend

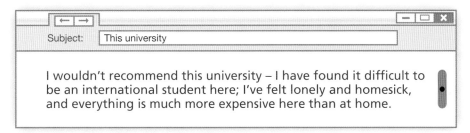

Subject: This university

I wouldn't recommend this university – I have found it difficult to be an international student here; I've felt lonely and homesick, and everything is much more expensive here than at home.

D: A commentator on social media

> Why should young people from this country have to compete for university places with international students? Why don't they go to university in their own countries? If you agree, please like, share and repost this.

The purpose of a source can be a strength or a limitation. Purpose is about the reason why a source has been made. Sometimes that purpose may point towards bias.

3   **a)** What do you think the purpose is of each of the four sources about international students?

    b) You have been asked this question: 'Is it better to study at university in your own country or travel to another country to study?' How might the purpose of each of the four sources affect how reliable it was for this question?

Developing

If we say a source is more **credible** than another, we mean it is convincing. In other words, it is well reasoned or evidenced, rather than just stated assertively or persuasively.

4 Compare these three sources for this question: 'Who is to **blame** for "brain drain" from African countries?' Then answer the questions below.

Source A: A cartoon from 2002 by Godfrey Mwampembwa, who signs his political cartoons as 'Gado'. Gado is from Tanzania and works for *The Eastern Standard* newspaper in Nairobi, Kenya.

Source: Gado.

Source C: Infographic on the brain drain in Kenya from an online business article, using data from international organisations and Kenyan universities.

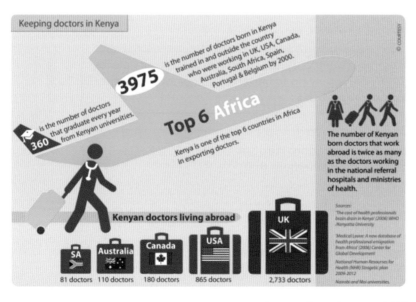

Source: *Smart Investor*, 2015.

Key terms

credible: convincing, persuasive; something people can believe in

Vocabulary

blame: to accuse someone of doing something wrong

brain drain: when highly educated people from one country migrate to another where there are better opportunities for them

compensate: to pay someone for something they have lost

lured: tempt someone by offering them an incentive

Source B: Christopher Mutsvangwa, a politician and spokesperson for ZANU-PF, the ruling party of Zimbabwe, in a speech in January 2022 as Minister for Media.

"The brain drain […] is done by the western countries because they do not train their people. […] Then when a crisis comes, they come to recruit from Zimbabwe because we are relatively poorer than them as we were enslaved and not as rich as they are. We trained people, they then come and snatch them.

They never want to **compensate** us for those people who take their money to train but they are now **lured** by better salaries."

a) What answer does each source suggest to you to the question, 'Who is to blame for "brain drain" from African countries?'

b) Complete a table like this one to describe the type, the author and the purpose of each of the three sources.

Source	Type of source	Author	Purpose
Source A	Political cartoon from 2002		
Source B		Government official	
Source C			To present information from a survey in a way that makes it easy to read

c) Which author do you think is most credible and which one least credible. Why?

d) Which purpose do you think is most credible and which one least credible. Why?

Final task

5 Evaluate the credibility of Sources A–C for answering the question: 'Who is to blame for "brain drain" from African countries?' Your answer should have the following structure:

Paragraph 1: State what each source suggests is the answer to the question, 'Who is to blame for "brain drain" from African countries?'

Paragraph 2: Consider the strengths and limitations of all three sources.

Paragraph 3: End by making a judgement about which source you consider most credible, giving the reasons for your decision.

Use the 'Checklist for success' to help you assess the credibility of sources.

Checklist for success

Sources can be considered credible when:

✔ the source and any data it contains is up to date

✔ the source of the evidence is clear

✔ the evidence is presented in a fair and neutral way

✔ the source is trustworthy and has a good track record

✔ the ideas offered are supported by other sources.

6 Display your evaluation as part of a class display. Read each other's evaluations. Make a note of:

• what worked well

• what worked less well

• what you would do to improve your evaluation next time.

Discuss your findings as a class.

❓ REFLECTION POINT

'All sources are useful for something, even biased ones.' What are biased sources useful for, and how would you need to use them?

What have you learned already in school about persuasive writing and how to structure an argument? Make a note of what you can remember.

Effective arguments about migration

Skills focus
✓ Evaluation

Learning focus
- To understand how the structure of an argument can make it more effective.
- To consider how evidence can make an argument more effective.

Big question: What makes some arguments about migration more effective than others?

Getting started

1 Here is a list of techniques for making arguments more persuasive.

a) Research (or recap) what the techniques involve and how to use them persuasively.

b) You could make your findings into a poster to display on the classroom wall.

rhetorical question	metaphor
alliteration	repetition
triplets	direct address
anecdote	

Exploring

2 Read this article from a website about migrants in the European Union (EU).

Imagine you are an editor for this website. Your boss thinks the points this article is making are good, but the order of the paragraphs needs more work. Your job is to re-structure the article so its argument is clearer and more convincing. Your boss says you can:

a) Move paragraphs around

b) Cut any text that you think is not relevant, is unclear or is repetitive

c) Add new text to make the argument 'flow' more easily.

Vocabulary

benefits: help given by the state, such as payments given to people who have lost their jobs

ageing population: when older people make up a bigger share of the population of a country than they used to

locally sourced: ingredients from the local area rather than from other regions or countries

essential workers: also called key workers; people who do jobs that are essential for society to function normally, such as nurses, cleaners and police

Look for ways to include some of the persuasive techniques you researched in the 'Getting started' activity.

Migrants in the European Union (EU)

According to Organisation for Economic Co-operation and Development (OECD), migrants to the EU contribute more in taxes than they receive in **benefits**, boost the numbers of people of working age (very important in countries with an **ageing population**) and arrive with skills and ambitions that contribute to technological progress.

Just one of hundreds of migrant success stories is that of Ibrahim Songne, who came to Italy from Burkina Faso as a young boy. Despite hating pizza the first time he tried it, Ibrahim's first job in a pastry shop inspired him to learn how to make pizza. He went on to open his own pizzeria in his home city of Trento, specialising in pizzas with crunchy bases and **locally sourced**, experimental toppings. By the time he was 30, his pizzeria IBRIS had been named one of the top 50 pizzerias in the world!

The 'Welcome and Thank you!' campaign to pass on positive and memorable migrant stories is starting in three European countries today: France, Italy and Germany. Currently 6 million people live in Germany who have migrated from outside the EU, 4 million in Italy and 4 million in France.

As well as the website, which is funded by the European Union as part of its Migration and Development Policy, there will be radio programmes on public radio stations – also available for listeners as podcasts.

As well as bringing fresh ideas and the determination to do well, European citizens rely on migrants for many essential but low-paid services. Thirteen per cent of **essential workers** in the EU are immigrants – and that percentage is much higher in some jobs: a third of cleaners are from outside the EU, for example.

All round the world, migrants bring big benefits to their new home countries. And yet, media coverage too often focuses on negative narratives about migration. The EU's new campaign aims to tackle this lack of balance.

Ibrahim's story is not at all rare: in fact, 21 per cent of those starting new businesses in the EU are migrants, creating thousands of new jobs.

Ibrahim Songne, owner IBRIS pizzeria, Trento.

Source: NPR website, 30 January 2022.

Developing

3 Your boss likes your revised version of the article very much – so much, in fact, that they want to enter it for a journalism prize!

The prize committee has a marking grid for evaluating non-fiction entries, which looks like this. Notes have been added to help the judges remember the different criteria.

Evaluation criteria	What to look for	Score 1–5 (where 1 is poor, 3 is average and 5 is excellent)
Use of evidence	Points in the article are backed up by reliable, relevant statistical evidence	
Reasoning	Points in the article are presented in a logical order to create an effective argument. There is no irrelevant or inconsistent information.	
Structure	There is a clear and coherent structure, which makes the article easy to read.	
Language	Language is precise and cautious, not vague or exaggerated.	

Copy and complete the first and third columns of the grid to evaluate a revised version of the article: it can be your own version or a partner's. Suggest areas for improvement before the article is sent to the judges!

4 **a)** Read this blog post about successful essay writing.

My 7 tips for essays that really work

I use this approach for all my essays – it has never failed me yet!

1. Start with an opening statement – say what your argument is going to be.

2. For each paragraph, use Point, Evidence, Explain. That means make a point, back it up with relevant evidence and explain how it strengthens your argument.

3. Include a perspective that argues against yours. Show you have considered it fairly and then explain why it does not fully convince you.

4. Be clear and concise – don't repeat yourself. Try to avoid long and complex sentences.

5. Use persuasive vocabulary in your writing such as: 'I am certain that…', 'for example…', 'as you can see…', 'for these reasons…', 'in fact…'.

6. Use vocabulary that helps you to be clear in your writing, such as 'My first point is…', 'A strength of this argument is…', 'In addition…'.

7. End with a conclusion that states your perspective again and repeats the main reasons for it.

b) Use the blog post plus what you have learned so far in this unit to write an effective argument about the benefits and challenges of migration. Your argument should:

- Use relevant evidence to make your argument more effective – remember the 'Point, Evidence, Explain' tip: make a point and then back it up with evidence

- Have an effective structure – remember to introduce what you are going to argue in the first paragraph, and end with a conclusion that sums up your argument, with paragraphs in between that set out your reasoning clearly and coherently

- Use precise (not vague), measured (not exaggerated) language plus persuasive techniques and vocabulary

- Avoid bias by including a perspective that argues against yours – show how you have considered it fairly and then explain why it does not fully convince you.

> **❓ REFLECTION POINT**
> Which is more important, would you say, for making a convincing argument: relevant statistical evidence or a clear and coherent structure? Explain your thinking.

Applying what you have learned

Skills focus
✓ Evaluation
Learning focus
• Evaluate the effectiveness of arguments.

Your task

You will prepare for and carry out a debate on the statement: 'Migration has more advantages than disadvantages.'

There are two sides to the debate. One side will argue for the statement – that migration has more advantages than disadvantages. The other side will argue against the statement – that migration has more disadvantages than advantages.

Approaching the task

A debate is all about how convincing, persuasive and effective you can make your argument. You may not personally agree with the argument your side has been given to make – that is something you have to put to one side, so you can focus on constructing your winning argument!

Your teacher will put you in a group and give you time to prepare your argument. You should work as a team to look through everything you have studied on migration, which could help you make a strong argument.

A debate has a strong structure. There are different ways of holding a debate, but a common one is like this:

- The side speaking for the statement goes first. They have two minutes to make their argument.

- The side speaking against the statement goes next. They have two minutes to make their argument.

- Then there is a two-minute break in which both sides come up with a counterargument or rebuttal. This is a statement about why the other side's argument is weaker than theirs!

- The side speaking against the statement goes first with two minutes to make their rebuttal and summarise their argument.

- Then the side speaking for the statement does their rebuttal and gives their final summary – two minutes.

So who wins? Simple – the rest of the class votes as to which side made the most convincing argument.

As you can see from how a debate works, you need evidence for your argument, but you also need to anticipate what the other side will argue against you. What evidence might they use? How would you counter their arguments and their evidence? You can take your notes into the debate, but two minutes is not very long to prepare a rebuttal, so it helps to have planned ahead.

As well as convincing facts, remember the tips for effective structure – point, evidence, explain works just as well for spoken arguments as for written ones, as does persuasive vocabulary. Most of the persuasive techniques you have studied were first developed for use in spoken arguments, so they are particularly effective in debates.

Different people in your group should speak in the debate: for making the argument, delivering the rebuttal and giving the summary. Different voices add engagement and interest for the audience. But don't waste time handing over to the next speaker – two minutes pass quickly!

Use the 'Checklist for success' to help you speak in a debate.

Checklist for success

✔ Rehearse your opening statement: a confident start will help to convince your audience.

✔ Don't make personal attacks on your opponents or try to put them off: debates should be won by the strongest, most convincing argument.

✔ Assertions are less convincing than statements backed up by relevant evidence.

✔ Anticipate the arguments your opponents are likely to use and prepare counterarguments.

What is your teacher looking for?

Your teacher is looking to see that you can:

- identify the strengths and limitations of sources and evidence

- discuss the effectiveness of arguments based on their structure and use of evidence.

Reflecting on your progress

Look at the 'Check your progress' on the next page and independently assess your learning. Then, with a partner, discuss:

- any new skills you have learned

- what you need to improve

- how the process has helped you to develop your thinking about this issue.

Check your progress

Beginning	Developing	Going beyond
• I can recognise that people think different things about an issue.	• I can identify some key points from different perspectives on the same issue within a source.	• I can identify ideas and evidence from different perspectives within different sources.
• I can draw conclusions from different types of evidence.	• I can find and interpret patterns in data.	• I can explain how evidence supports an argument or a perspective.
• I can discuss a source, and say what the author's ideas are about an issue.	• I can discuss a source, considering the author or purpose, and use this to comment on its strengths and limitations.	• I can evaluate sources, considering the author and purpose, recognising that some sources may be more credible than others.
• I can give my opinion about another person's ideas on an issue, with reasons for my opinion.	• I can discuss my own opinion about someone else's perspective, identifying points I agree or disagree with.	• I can discuss the effectiveness of an argument in terms of its structure and use of evidence.
• I can use some persuasive techniques in my writing.	• I can use a range of persuasive techniques to support my arguments.	• I can strengthen my arguments by using a range of persuasive techniques successfully.

Next steps

Does your school have a debating club that you could join to develop your debating skills? If not, could you start one? What would your first debating issue be?

What migrant stories are connected to your school and/or to your local area? You could carry out some research locally and create a class display about migration. You could also visit the library or research online to find out about people from your local area who have migrated to different countries.

Improving your work in groups or teams

Changing communities

5

The spectacular snow and ice festival shown in the image is a source of much pride to the community who produces it. Understanding the community that we live in is a first step in knowing how to celebrate it. Our community is central to our development, both educationally and socially. But what do we really know about our community? How has it changed? How do we celebrate the things that make it special?

In this chapter, you will be exploring the topic of 'Change in culture and communities', thinking about the following issues:

- **How do local communities celebrate their identity through food?**
- **How do teams work together to make festivals a success?**
- **How can you be a leader and part of a team at the same time?**
- **How can team members persuade others to support their 'big idea'?**
- **Should you take care of your own performance or put your team first?**

You will be developing a range of research, reflection and collaboration skills:

5.1 Reviewing your research skills

5.2 Collaborating positively

5.3 Using team roles effectively

5.4 Creating an effective team outcome

5.5 Reflecting on your team's performance

5.6 Applying what you have learned.

Your final task will be to write a personal reflection on your individual contribution to your group's preparation and presentation.

Reviewing your research skills

Skills focus
✓ Research
Learning focus
- Identify appropriate sources to answer a research question.
- Conduct and record research into your chosen topic or issue.

Big question: How do local communities celebrate their identity through food?

Getting started

Some types of food are often strongly linked to places or regions around the world.

1 Working with a partner, discuss these food items. Do you know what they are, and where they come from? (Some of them are not as obvious as you think.) How would you find out more?

Key lime pie	Tangerine
Jollof rice	Arborio rice
Black Forest gateau	

Exploring

To research the big question – 'How do local communities celebrate their identity through food?' – you need to start by identifying the key words in the question:

- *How* = in what ways, by doing what?
- *local communities* = communities based around villages, towns, cities or small regions
- *celebrate* = promote and present with pride
- *identity* = what makes them special/unique?
- *food* = food is the focus (not, for example, sport or fashion).

2 Consider these sources for research:

i) A recipe book for food from your country

ii) A tourist guide website about an olive festival on an island

iii) Your conversation with an older person about local community events they went to when they were younger

iv) A programme for a local community's music festival

v) A book called *Food festivals around the world*

vi) An online interview with a local chef saying what they love about local food

vii) Attending a food festival yourself.

a) Put the sources in order of priority of how well they match what you are trying to find out.

b) Write down your rank order from 1 (best match) to 7 (least good match).

c) Explain briefly why each source would be useful or not so useful. Think carefully – you may find out unexpectedly useful things from some sources.

3 Remember that sources can be **primary** or **secondary**. Which of the above is likely to be primary and which secondary sources?

Developing

To check that the source you identified has the information you need, you must ask the right questions.

4 Imagine you had chosen Source ii – a tourist guide website about an olive festival on an island – as being useful.

Here are two of the questions you want answers to. Note down *at least two more* questions you want to answer using the source.

1. What is the name of the festival and where does it take place?
2. When does it happen?

....

....

5 Now read this extract from the source.

> The Olive Festival takes place every year in the aptly named village of Zeytinlik, which means 'the place of olives', located in Kyrenia. Home to countless olive trees for centuries, the region is still a source of the island's olive supply to this day.
>
> The festival itself? A week of fun and **frivolity**! Typically taking place within the first week of October, it sees the **tranquil** village of Zeytinlik transform into an entertainment hub with hundreds of visitors flocking in from all corners of the island to join the celebrations. It is a perfect opportunity for the locals to **showcase** their skills – not only in the form of delicious food (credits to olive oil, no less) but also impressive **handicrafts** such as jewellery, pottery and many other traditional home decorations! Of course, the festival wouldn't be complete without some live music and **folklore** dancing!
>
> The celebrations aren't always just limited to Zeytinlik village itself. The enthusiasm usually continues at the Kyrenia **amphitheatre** by the harbour, which hosts concerts by popular singers in honour of the festival. It is also **customary** for olive factories to open their doors to visitors who want to experience the very process of making olive oil first-hand!

Source: Cyprus Paradise.

🔑 Key terms

primary source: original material, for example raw data or a first-hand account, such as a diary entry or interview

secondary source: material that draws on and interprets primary sources, such as articles and reports or graphs and tables based on collected data

Vocabulary

frivolity: light-hearted behaviour

tranquil: calm

showcase: to display something in public in order to show off its good features

handicrafts: hand-made decorative objects

folklore: traditional beliefs, customs or stories

amphitheatre: large outdoor space where plays are performed

customary: traditional or normal practice

6 Make notes on the tourist guide website by jotting down:

- what you have found out about this local olive festival
- what the festival reveals about the community and its history.

For example, you might note:

> Takes place in village with name of festival food!
> Olives still grown here.
>
> Happens (usually) first week in October
>
> Pride in drawing in 'hundreds of visitors'

7 Is this source suitable for answering the big question at the start of the unit: 'How do local communities celebrate their identity through food?' Discuss your view with a partner.

Final task

At the end of this chapter, your task will be to work in a group to present your ideas for a festival to celebrate or introduce your school community and perhaps the cultures in it.

Your group will conduct local research to answer these questions:

- What cultures or backgrounds do young people in your school have? Do they come from the same nations, regions or ethnic groups?
- What particular interests do young people in your school have? For example, are there specific crafts or foods they would like to celebrate? Or are they proud of other things such as music, clothes, literature or sport in their community?
- In what ways (if at all) has the local school community changed over time? (For example, has it grown? Does it include more varied cultures?)
- If there are lots of different cultures in your school community, what do the young people there share? For example, are there shared values to celebrate, such as kindness, tolerance, being inclusive and celebrating difference?

You will also need to look outside your local community to consider how other cultures and communities (national or global) celebrate their interests and **heritage**.

Vocabulary

heritage: valued cultural traditions, objects or practices passed down from previous generations

8 Working in your group, divide up the local research task by allocating a group (source of information) from the list below to each member. If one of these requires more attention, then you can always work in pairs.

- Students at your school, or other local schools

- Family members, carers or friends

- School teachers or other staff

- Wider groups and cultures (for example, through online research)

- Anyone else who you think might have a perspective on what a good school festival might celebrate.

9 Decide what research method you will use to find out more from your chosen source – for example, will you use primary research methods, such as a simple questionnaire or a more structured interview? Or will you need to carry out secondary research? Or will you need to use both primary and secondary research?

❓ REFLECTION POINT

Revisit the questions under 'Final task' and write your own answers to them. You could use the following prompts to help you structure your ideas.

I have a particular interest in…

My own culture is represented by…

I have/haven't attended festivals that represent…

I would like to see…because this would show…

Viewing the cherry blossom (Hanami) is a traditional annual celebration in Japan.

Collaborating positively

Skills focus
✓ Collaboration
Learning focus
- Work positively in your team towards a shared outcome.
- Develop techniques to encourage others and tackle disagreements.

Big question: How do teams work together to make festivals a success?

Getting started

Perhaps you have heard about – or even attended – the Harbin Snow and Ice Festival.

1 Working with a partner, discuss:

a) What are the workers in the photo collaborating to do?

b) Why do you think the people who organised this festival chose snow and ice to celebrate?

c) Do you think it would be of interest to only local people, or to others as well? Why?

The Snow and Ice Festival in the city of Harbin, China.

Exploring

Collaborating positively is very important, not just for huge festivals such as the Harbin Snow and Ice Festival, but for much smaller events and tasks.

By this stage in your school career, you will have worked as part of a team, both in Global Perspectives lessons and in other subject areas – so what does 'collaborating positively' mean to you?

2 Think about this way of working and jot down your own definitions. For example:

> Collaborating positively means…
>
> – Working towards the same goal
>
> – Making sure we…

3 Working in a small group, share your ideas about what collaborating positively means. Between you, create a simple group poster with *five* agreed key pointers that you think everyone should bear in mind when working together.

In the last unit, you were individually tasked with doing some research into local interests and cultures. Your research should have generated some ideas. You now have a chance to firm those ideas up.

4 In your group, share any information that you found out related to individual or local interests and cultures in your area.

  a) What did you find out?

  b) Was there anything that was surprising or new to you?

  c) Which, if any, of these do you think would be of interest beyond your local community? Why?

  d) How did the information change (or reinforce) the way you view your school or local community?

5 After you have shared this initial research, spend 5 minutes working on your own reflecting on how well you worked together as a group. Jot down answers to these questions:

  a) Did everyone get a chance to contribute? Why?

  b) How positive was the discussion? Did you and other group members encourage others or prompt them for more information?

  c) Is there anything you, or your group, should do differently next time you share ideas?

Developing

By now, you will have quite a lot of information about the different interests and cultures of your community. You have also seen how two communities celebrate local interest or tradition (olives and snow/ice) and how these might be of interest to others, such as tourists.

6 In your group, create a **mood board** of some of the different interests and cultural aspects represented in your community. This could include photos, key words, **found objects** (such as bits of cloth, food packets) or fragments of texts such as poems/songs.

For each item or image, write a simple label to go with it. For example:

This is the favourite sweet eaten by teenagers in our school.

This is Tia skateboarding in our central park.

7 In your group, discuss how your own festival could represent your chosen community in a positive way. It does not need to be a huge, expensive festival, but it does need to be one that your class or school community could put on.

Discuss your responses to the questions below.

a) What would your main **concept** be?

- Would it be lots of different things or would it have a narrower focus, such as food, sports or local arts/crafts?
- Would your festival have a name?

b) How might it look or be organised?

- Would it take place over one afternoon or a longer time?
- Where and when would it happen?
- Would it have stalls, presentations, performances?
- Would it be an online festival or have an online element?

c) How would the festival be **marketed** or promoted?

- Will you send out **press releases** or promotional leaflets?
- Will you record video posts, or create posters or advertisements?

d) What might the health and safety issues be?

- Who might you need to talk to or inform about the festival?
- How might this change or affect what you wish to do?

e) What would the costs be?

- How can you estimate costs?
- Would you charge for anything, such as entrance tickets?
- Would you look for sponsorship? If so, from whom?

f) How will you measure its success?

- How could you find out what people thought of the festival?
- Would you have 'on the spot' interviews with participants and attendees during the event? Or would you send out surveys and questionnaires afterwards?

National Aboriginal Day and Indigenous Arts Festival, Toronto, Canada

Vocabulary

concept: overall plan, idea or intention

marketed: advertised or promoted

press release: official statement about an event given to the media

Final task

8 Once you have agreed the basic concept for your festival, write up your ideas in the form of a proposal. For now, this will be just a working document that you will refer to later in the chapter.

- Each group must have a proposal – and each member of the group should have a copy of it.

- Use the template below to help you. It includes an example that has been started by a group at another school.

The name of our festival	The Meadway Eastern Arts and Crafts Festival
The concept/big idea	A celebration of some of the amazing arts and crafts done by our school students, as the school has a large Japanese community, among other East Asian backgrounds. The festival will showcase talented people producing arts and crafts that reflect their culture and community.
How it will be organised	There will be a series of workshops in the main school hall over one Saturday afternoon: – a Manga workshop, run by one of our students, Anna, whose mum is Japanese – a Reiki pottery demonstration (another Japanese art form) – wicker basket making.
How it will be marketed/promoted	Advertise using posters around school. Send out emails to parents/families.
Health and safety	Carry out a risk assessment of hall with the Deputy Head. Complete a risk assessment form downloaded from the internet.
Costs	We will seek sponsorship from local businesses.
How to measure success	We will survey everyone as they leave the festival.

❓ REFLECTION POINT

What do you think are the biggest opportunities and challenges in putting on such a festival? How could planning play an important role?

Note down any action points you could bring back to the group at your next team meeting.

Using team roles effectively

Skills focus
✓ Collaboration
Learning focus
- Understand how different types of roles are important for a team.
- Use your skills to take on a positive role in the team.

Big question: How can you be a leader and part of a team at the same time?

Getting started

There are lots of different verbs that represent both thinking and doing in school. Some of these are shown in the word cloud.

> think present discuss explain argue
> persuade explore analyse consider practise
> memorise find out copy describe

These verbs can be demonstrated through speech, writing or movement – or a combination of these.

1 Working with a partner, come up with one example for each of these verbs that you have demonstrated in school (for example, copying a move in sport, or explaining a process in science).

Exploring

What the activity above should show is that while we may think of ourselves as a particular *type* of person (a 'thinker' or a 'doer', say), in fact we are all able to play many roles. It is true that in a team, some people will feel more comfortable in one role than another. But equally, it is important that you try to improve in those roles you find more challenging.

For example, all group members can develop leadership skills that will benefit both the individual and the group.

2 Which of the leadership skills on the next page do you have? Copy and complete the table, adding examples, where you can, of when you have demonstrated each skill.

Leadership skill	Example
Sets goals for own work or for groupwork, and monitors own, or others', progress	My goal was to improve the quality of the notes I make. Follow-up: I used a table with headings when I researched the olive festival.
Shows discipline by keeping to deadlines both in life (for example, with friends or family) or at school	
Anticipates problems and is **proactive** (for example, prepares for issues or obstacles when planning)	
Sets an example through how you collaborate and interact with others	
Can be friendly, approachable and encouraging	
Can motivate others to achieve	
An intelligent listener: open to ideas/feedback, and able to 'read' people's words and actions	
Can keep the team's best interests in mind rather than just their own	

Developing

As well as being a leader by example, there are some specific group roles you need to consider for various stages of your project. For example:

- *Ideas contributor*: everyone needs to take on this role, especially at the start of the process.

- *Note-taker*: you will all have to keep your own notes, but for the big decisions, as you discuss and **refine** your ideas, it is useful to have someone who can record what you decide and any actions to be taken. This role can rotate around each group member.

- *Chairperson*: this is someone who guides and directs your meetings. Again, this role can be done by a different group member for each meeting, but it needs to be someone who is firm, can keep the group on track, stick to an **agenda** (if you have one) and make sure everyone gets their say.

3 Read through this possible agenda for your next meeting.

Can you think of any other roles you might need to address when presenting your concept? Jot them down.

> Group meeting, Lesson 3
> 1. Recap what sort of festival we are planning and our **rationale**
> 2. The presentation – allocation of jobs
> 3. Next steps/actions

> **Vocabulary**
>
> **rationale**: reasons for doing something

The allocation of jobs could include:

- Presenter – explains the big idea/concept and key reasons for the festival

- Promoter/marketer – explains how the festival will be promoted

- Finance officer – explains costs and how they will be covered

- Health and safety officer – explains how risks will be addressed

- Evaluator/assessor – explains how the success of the festival will be measured.

4 Now make notes in answer to these questions:

a) Which of the jobs above appeals to you most?

b) Which would suit you best bearing in mind your personality and skill set?

c) Which would you like to take on even if they are out of your comfort zone, to develop your skill set?

5 One student has kept a reflective log, noting down how well her own team assigned roles for a mini festival they were working on.

Read through the log, then discuss these questions with a partner:

a) In what ways did the group work collaboratively at first?

b) In what way did the group *not* succeed at first?

c) How did the group rectify the problem?

d) What did they learn?

e) How could they have helped Evie develop her skill set?

We talked through all the roles we'd like to do, and then jointly voted for each person (where there was more than one who was keen). For example, Tasha wanted to take on the role of accountant as she is very good at mathematics and has a logical mind. She talked through some of the likely costs she predicted. She had already produced a simple spreadsheet. However, Evie was very persuasive and said she had organised a charity fun run, so was well-prepared for doing this, so this persuaded us to choose her. But, when we met next time, Evie didn't have any figures and wasn't able to present a clear spreadsheet, so it was agreed that Tasha would be more suitable for this role. Evie agreed to take on marketing. We probably should have spent more time at the start considering who had appropriate experience for each role rather than just listening to who was loudest and most confident or keen.

Final task

6 As a group, look again at the short three-point agenda in question 3.

Then, run a 15–20-minute discussion to help you prepare for the presentation.

Read through the 'Checklist for success' to give you some tips.

Checklist for success

✔ Decide on some basic roles for the meeting, for example chairperson, note-taker (you will all need to contribute ideas!).

✔ Discuss and decide who will take on what job (for example, presenter, marketer) for the presentation.

✔ Put into practice everything you have learned about positive collaboration and being a leader.

✔ Set goals or next steps.

❷ REFLECTION POINT

When the discussion has finished, create a simple voice note or recording (on your phone if you have one) explaining:

- how you fulfilled a role or roles in the group
- how you led and shared responsibilities
- what job you are taking on – and why.

Creating an effective team outcome

Big question: How can team members persuade others to support their 'big idea'?

Getting started

Have you heard of a programme that started in Japan called *The Tigers of Money?* In the UK, it was renamed *Dragon's Den*. In it, **entrepreneurs** **pitch** a business idea to a group of wealthy **investors** based on their research into **gaps in the market**. If the investors (called 'dragons' or 'tigers' because they can be frightening) like the idea, they offer money for a **share** in the business.

1. Here are some business ideas. Which one do you think was successful in *Dragon's Den?* Which one was real, but unsuccessful? And which one is completely made up? Discuss each one with a partner.

   - *The Drive Safe Glove* – a single glove you put on your right or left hand to remind you which side of the road to drive on.

   - *Wonderbly* – a company that produces individual picture books in which the buyer's own children feature in the stories.

   - *Cat Mini* – a tiny version of the Mini car, designed for cats to drive around the garden.

Exploring

There are many ways to pitch your ideas for your school community festival. But whatever method you choose, it will need to be:

- a group presentation, agreed by all of you, in which you all participate, taking on the jobs agreed in Unit 5.3

- clear and persuasive, supported by evidence or good reasons.

Vocabulary

den: a wild animal's home

entrepreneur: a person who sets up their own business

pitch: put forward or propose an idea

investors: people who lend or put money into businesses

gaps in the market: opportunities to sell something new to people

share: a part in the ownership (of a business)

think outside the box: a metaphor that means coming up with unusual or original ideas

Here are some ideas of the sorts of things you could include (in addition to verbally presenting).

Some of these suggestions might seem a bit strange, but it is useful to '**think outside the box**' in terms of how you persuade your teacher (or whoever the 'tiger/dragon' is). For example, you could start a presentation about a food festival with a tasting quiz.

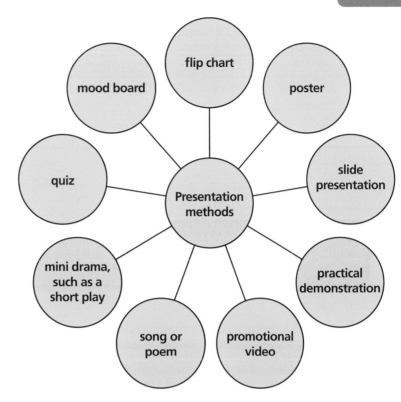

2 In your group, discuss how you might fit supporting resources or activities into your presentation.

3 Once you have settled on an idea, in discussion with your group, create a plan for your presentation. As a minimum, make sure it records who is doing what, and any resources you need.

You could record your plan in a table like the one below.

Stages and timings	Who/what	Resources
Introduction (1 minute)	Lena sums up the concept and uses instant quiz to engage interest.	n/a
Part 1 (2 minutes)	Evie explains marketing ideas: festival based on research into people's cultures, food choices and why these mean so much.	Slide show, slides 1–3 show different foods
Part 2 (3 minutes)	Tasha explains costs: for example, food, promotion, stands, and so on.	Slide show, slides 3–4 show simple spreadsheet with accounts
Part 3 (3 minutes)	Mia explains how health and safety will be addressed.	n/a
Conclusion (1 minute)	Lena gives details: date; how it will celebrate community; how success will be measured.	Give out leaflet promoting festival

Checklist for success

Remember to appoint someone:

✔ to chair your discussion

✔ to keep notes and a record of any decisions you make.

Developing

What makes a persuasive presentation? Think about the language you use to support your ideas. For example:

- Language you use to organise the information you present:
    - Firstly, secondly, ...
    - Next, following on from, later...
    - When, while, during...
    - Finally, ultimately, to finish off...
- Language you use to give reasons:
    - We want to celebrate...*because* that tells us a lot about...
    - *As a result of* our research, we decided to...
- Language you use to refer to sources or visuals:
    - We *found out* that..., Our research *revealed* that..., We *concluded* that...
    - We *identified*..., We *discovered*..., We *observed* that..., We *learned* that...
    - *According to*..., *As this graph/table shows*...

4 a) Work with someone from another group to present your group's ideas as clearly and effectively as possible to each other.

- Use as many of the phrases above that will fit what you are saying.
- Think about how you can use non-verbal gestures such as smiling, opening the palms of your hands as if to explain, etc., to support what you say.
- Remember, this is not your presentation – just a 'practice run' at trying out some of the language you could use.

Take it in turns to:

- Introduce your festival idea/concept
- Explain the background to your idea, the research you did and what it revealed
- Give reasons why you chose the idea
- Make notes as the other person presents.

b) Then, give each other feedback on the idea. Effective feedback means:

- Be specific and avoid generalisations (don't just say 'you spoke well', instead say 'you linked your main idea to your research')
- Check you have understood correctly (for example, by saying, 'So, if I have got this right, you're planning to...').

5 Return to your group and discuss the feedback you received. If necessary, refine your group's festival idea, taking on board what was said.

Final task

6 In your group, work together to create your presentation about your festival idea. The presentation should last no more than 10 minutes, including any audio, video or other supporting material you wish to use.

Once you have developed your presentation, conduct a full rehearsal, possibly with someone recording it.

You will perform your presentation at the start of the next unit.

Language support

In any presentations you do, consider the tone, pace and pitch of your voice. You might want to:

- raise your pitch or speed up to create momentum or excitement

- slow down and lower your voice for a more serious or reflective point.

Read the 'Checklist for success' to help you with your group presentation.

Checklist for success

✔ Agree a group plan for the presentation. This should include a running order (who speaks and in what order).

✔ Work collaboratively to produce any resources you need (this will probably require additional time outside this lesson).

✔ Link your festival idea to the research you did.

✔ Use suitable connecting words and phrases to persuade, and to support and order your points.

❓ REFLECTION POINT

As a group, look at what you did and share ideas about how effective it was and where it might be improved. Refine the idea, then practise the presentation one more time before presenting it for real in the next unit.

Reflecting on your team's performance

Skills focus
✓ Reflection

Learning focus
* Reflect on what you learned about teamwork.
* Comment on the benefits and challenges you experienced.

Big question: Should you take care of your own performance or put your team first?

Getting started

There is usually an assumption that a great team is better than a group of individuals. However, there are challenges and difficulties when working together. It is important to try to identify what those challenges are, but also to celebrate the things that go well.

1   The scientist Isaac Newton is credited with discovering how gravity works. He said, 'If I have seen further, it is by standing on the shoulders of giants.' This was an **analogy** he used to express something about his own achievements.

   a) What do you think Isaac Newton meant?

   b) Do you think he is right?

   c) Discuss the quotation with a partner and try to put it into your own words.

> 🔑 **Key term**
>
> **analogy**: a comparison made between two things in order to explain or clarify

Exploring

2   You will start this unit by giving your group's presentation to the class (or whatever audience your teacher has decided upon).

* Remember the core presentation skills you developed in the last unit.

* Equally, try to observe and keep a mental note on *how* the presentation goes.

3   Now reflect more widely on your group's overall performance, both in developing and giving the presentation. To do this:

   a) Read through the success criteria in the table on the next page.

   b) Copy and complete the table, noting down *at least one* example of where your group (team) achieved each criterion (where you can).

Success criteria In our team, we...	Example of how team achieved this
Shared the workload by...	
Discussed and developed ideas when...	
Learned from each other when...	
Solved problems together by...	
Enjoyed working as a team because...	
Saw or understood different perspectives in our team when...	
Supported or encouraged others in the team, for example when...	
Shared a group sense of achievement through...	

4 Were there any criteria for which you were unable to think of examples? If so, note down any reasons why these were *not* benefits you experienced. Consider:

- Was it because the opportunities didn't arise?
- Did members of the team make it difficult, for whatever reason?
- Or was this because of a different reason?

5 Read this reflection by a member of the team who presented ideas about a food festival.

The overall response to our presentation was excellent. Our teacher said it was well-planned, and that between us we had clearly covered all the main areas such as marketing and health and safety. Each member had played a part and worked hard leading up to the presentation.
I felt a sense of fulfilment because we had achieved what we set out to do. The others felt the same. And we all had a chance to participate. Jayden lacked confidence and didn't want to speak, but we practised with him before and he managed to say a small amount.
One thing that didn't go so well, was that I felt we didn't really take on board each other's ideas. The others weren't very interested in the cost aspects, which they could have referred to in their own parts of the presentation but didn't.

The most delicious event of this summer

FOODSTIVAL

27 july

Location address
www.foodstival.com

- FOOD FAIR
- LIVE MUSIC
- FAMILY FUN

FREE ADMISSION

6 Having read the student's reflection, working on your own, make a note of:

    a) Which of the eight success criteria (from the table above) were mentioned?

    b) Is there anything from the list of success criteria that didn't go so well or wasn't commented on?

Developing

When you reflect in this way, it helps to mention specific examples, rather than speaking in general terms. In the response above, the student is specific about what was 'well-planned' – they mention how they 'covered all the main areas such as marketing and health and safety'.

7 There is just one specific reference to another member of the group. Who does the response refer to and what is the reference made? Jot down your answer.

It is easier to provide specific examples when you have some clear phrases to guide your reflection.

8 Using the phrases in the table below, discuss in pairs your work towards and including the presentation. Aim to link the phrases to specific examples.

Achievements	Challenges/problems
• One thing that went well was…	• One thing that didn't go so well was…
• We managed to…, We were able to…	• We didn't manage to…, We were unable to…
• It was effective when…	• It was not so effective/ineffective when…
• An example of how things worked well was…	• An example of how things worked less well…
• A successful/positive element of…	• One challenge/problem was…

9 Write a reflection of 150–175 words on how well your team worked on this project. You could structure your reflection simply in the form of four sections, like this:

1. Introduction – the focus of the presentation: 'Our presentation proposed a festival about…'

2. Body text 1 – what went well: 'I think we managed to…', 'Another thing we did well is…'

3. Body text 2 – what didn't go so well: 'However, we struggled to…'

4. Conclusion – evaluation of success/challenge overall: 'On the whole/In general, I think we…'

Read the 'Checklist for success' to help you to write your reflection.

Checklist for success

✔ Comment on as many of the eight success criteria for the presentation (achieved or not achieved).

✔ Use some of the phrases from the table.

✔ Link your comments to specific examples of what went well or not so well.

✔ Remember to comment on the content: how the presentation evolved or changed and how well the final version represented the school community.

? REFLECTION POINT

Your reflection of your team's performance should enable you to pinpoint what you, as a team, could do better next time.

Working together, discuss and agree three commitments for how you could work better on a new project. Phrasing these as solid commitments, rather than more abstract 'hopes', is useful in ensuring you put them into practice.

Add these to your overall written reflection. For example:

In the future, we will ensure everyone speaks for the same amount of time in any presentation we do.

Applying what you have learned

Skills focus
✓ Reflection
Learning focus
- Reflect on your own personal performance within your team.
- Consider how your perspective on an issue has changed or developed.

Your task

You will write a personal reflection on your task to present ideas for a community festival. In this task, the focus is on you as an individual. Your reflection should include:

- what you knew or originally thought about the issue related to your school community

- how you contributed to the task of planning a festival and the presentation

- what particular skills you demonstrated well or found challenging

- what you learned about the issue – how it changed (if at all) your understanding of local communities and cultures

- how this might affect future work or research you do.

Approaching the task

1 Read this extract from a student's feedback. Working on your own, note down:

- which skills from the above list the student has demonstrated

- what else they could have expanded upon or included.

It was my job to find out about any arts and crafts interests in my year group. I started by sending out a simple questionnaire that asked students if they did any arts or crafts, and if these were linked to their family or cultural background. I think the research was effective because I got some good responses showing that animation was very popular. This led to me suggesting an animation workshop as part of the festival, which my group agreed would be interesting. I was able to express my idea clearly but, because I was not able to give a reason for including it in the festival, my group chose some other more traditional workshops such as basket-weaving, charcoal drawing and mask-making.

2 Read this extract from someone from the same group. In what ways is this a more effective response? Think about:

- their understanding of the issue at the start of the process
- what they say about working with others
- what skill they were able to show in the group discussion
- what they say they learned about their changing community.

> At the start, I understood that festivals such as the snow and ice festival in Harbin, China, created pride but also brought communities together. So, working cooperatively with a partner in my team, we researched our local community but discovered the old arts fair they used to have had stopped due to lack of interest. However, the community has changed now – and when we ran a survey in school, it revealed lots of new arts and crafts (some from other cultures) as well as digital animation, producing products using sustainable materials and so on. So, I showed confidence by persuading our group that our school festival should focus on these new crafts.
>
> I supported my perspective effectively by showing screenshots of school friends participating in their hobby or art, like two students who created a simple gaming app which they shared on the web with students from a school in the USA. As a result, I became more observant of my community: my research taught me that arts and crafts are not 'fixed' but develop over time as communities change. I think these must be celebrated, as it creates understanding of what people care about.

3 Write your own personal reflection of 175–200 words. Make sure you address each of the bullet points under 'Approaching the task'.

Reflecting on your progress

Using the 'Check your progress' bullets at the end of this chapter, evaluate your own performance and decide what you did effectively and what you might need to improve.

Check your progress

Beginning	Developing	Going beyond
• I understand what I am looking for when I conduct research.	• I can make sound judgements about which research sources are relevant.	• I can evaluate a range of sources and particular research methods.
• I understand what makes a positive collaboration or discussion.	• I can contribute positively to group discussions, including supporting others and showing positive leadership qualities.	• I can identify strengths and weaknesses of group discussion and act to improve it.
• I understand the ways in which I can be a leader within my group.		• I can take on roles outside my comfort zone and learn from them.
• I can work with my group to develop a project.	• I can contribute to multiple elements of a project and help improve its presentation.	• I can identify areas for improvement and refine ideas, including a range of responses.
• I understand what makes a successful team performance.	• I can evaluate how well my team met the expectations for effective teamwork.	• I can reflect on my team's performance, citing clear and specific examples.
• I can write about my individual performance, giving some basic examples of what I did well.	• I can address all four elements of the reflective cycle and comment reflectively.	• I can trace the development of my understanding of community and change.

Next steps

Create, design and illustrate your own 'Dos and Don'ts' list of guidance points for people working in groups.

Find out about a specific festival you would like to travel to and create a 'travel pack' of guidance on how to get there, where to stay and what to do and see. Include some thoughts or ideas on what you hope to find out about the local community and their traditions.

Researching ideas and analysing the evidence

Our digital world

6

Many aspects of our world are now digital, using computer technology in some way. Much of the way we communicate, the music we listen to, the news we read and the images we share are today created, transmitted and stored in digital form. This can make sharing our lives with others easier – but are these changes for the better? Can we trust every aspect of our digital world?

In this chapter, you will be exploring the topic of 'Digital world', thinking about the following issues:

- **How honest should we be when presenting ourselves online?**

- **What is the 'global village' – and is everyone part of it?**

- **Is learning better online or face to face?**

- **Is taking selfies selfish?**

- **Should we be excited or concerned by the 'internet of things'?**

You will be developing a range of research, analysis, reflection and communication skills:

6.1 Analysing ideas from different perspectives

6.2 Studying an issue and its consequences on others

6.3 Suggesting different actions as responses to a global issue

6.4 Reflecting on the impact of exploring different perspectives

6.5 Presenting evidence to support arguments

6.6 Applying what you have learned.

Your final task will be to research whether people tend to use the internet to share and develop their ideas only with those with similar views.

Analysing ideas from different perspectives

Skills focus
✓ Analysis

Learning focus
- Analyse ideas from different perspectives.
- Use different sources to explore ideas on a given issue.
- Understand how different perspectives may lead to different conclusions.

Big question: How honest should we be when presenting ourselves online?

Getting started

1 If you were taking part in an online video call, how would you want to appear to others?

a) Working on your own, complete a table like the one below.

	...for a job interview?	...with a group of friends?
How would you dress...		
What would you have in the background...		
How would you behave...		

b) With a partner, discuss your responses to these questions:

- What are you aiming to do when you make these choices?

- Is it okay to present yourself differently in different situations?

- If you did these things face to face rather than online, would you dress or behave differently?

In this unit, you are going to explore the way different people present themselves online. You will consider how these different presentations can lead to different conclusions.

Exploring

Some people make a profession out of being on public view. They, and their organisation, go to a lot of trouble to present a certain image.

2 **a)** Describe how this newsreader looks. What is your impression of him?

b) What is the purpose of the image on the right of the newsreader? How might this help to make the programme more effective?

c) What might you conclude about how the news organisation wants to be seen by its viewers?

CLIMATE CHANGE CRISIS
OCEANS ARE POLLUTED, THE AIR IS DIRTY   NEWS
DAILY REPORT THE NEW SMARTPHONE CHANGED THE WAY WE USE TECHNOLOGY NFTS

3 Now look at this image of a late-night chat show. Compare the way this studio is set up with the news programme.

a) What are the similarities? What are the differences? Suggest reasons for any differences.

b) What might you conclude about how the late-night chat show wants to be seen by its viewers?

One way of presenting yourself online is by creating an 'avatar' – a cartoon figure that represents you in a video game or on social media. Today, you can personalise your avatar in detail using apps.

4 The image on the left is Volha's avatar, which she uses on video games and social media. It is based on the photograph shown on the right.

In a small group, discuss these questions:

a) What impression do you get of Volha from her photo?

b) What impression do you get of Volha from her avatar?

c) What do Volha's choices communicate about how she wants to be seen online?

d) What do you think are the benefits of using an avatar to present yourself online? What disadvantages could there be? Make notes in two columns.

5 Winston and Ahmed are sharing views about how people appear online.

Winston

People are often dishonest when they appear online. You never get a true sense of what they look like or what they think.

It's not dishonest to want to look good. People naturally want to present themselves well and there's nothing wrong with that.

Ahmed

Working on your own:

a) Summarise the perspective each person has.

b) Do you mostly agree with Winston, or with Ahmed? Why?

c) Suggest why different perspectives may lead to different conclusions.

Developing

Below is an extract from a blog about how we present ourselves online, written by Josh Renyard, a media production student. Renyard used a questionnaire to research people's experiences and views of presenting themselves online.

6 **a)** Read the extract from the blog. Working on your own, summarise the perspective given by the people Renyard interviewed.

b) With a partner, discuss your responses to these questions:

- Do you think people are right to only present positive images of themselves online? What might be the consequences of this?

- What might be the effect of posting a less positive self-representation online?

- Can a person's representation of themselves online be realistic and accurate even if it isn't 'full'?

> **Vocabulary**
>
> **intrigued**: to feel curious about something and want to know more
>
> **curate**: to select, organise and present something, for example items in a museum or information online
>
> **false**: dishonest, inaccurate
>
> **representation**: an image of something, portrayed in a particular way
>
> **conscious**: deliberate
>
> **omission**: decision to leave something out

by Josh Renyard, 16 May 2019

Online image – how do we present ourselves online?

Something which has always **intrigued** me is how we present ourselves online compared to real life[...]. It is often thought, or assumed, that the offline version of ourselves is more 'real' than the online. The greater ability to control and **curate** what information about ourselves is visible lends itself to this ability to present a **false** version of ourselves[...].

From speaking to peers[...], I had come to understand that many of them do in fact curate their online images, choosing only to post images which they feel are their 'best looking' for example. However, it appears that many do not consider this to be a false **representation** of themselves[...].

So while many appear to be aware that what they post online about themselves is not a *full* representation, they still consider it to be realistic and accurate, despite the **conscious omission** of particular elements.

Source: Josh Renyard blog

This is an extract from an online article about the benefits of being yourself online. The article describes the results of an experiment involving social media users.

---

www.ScientificAmerican…

The benefits of being yourself online   by Erica R. Bailey and Sandra Matz

For this experiment, we **recruited** social media users and **randomly assigned** them to either post in a way that was **authentic** (based on their personality) or post in a way that was popular and made them look good in the eyes of others.

After a week spent following these instructions, we switched the groups: the people who had initially posted in an authentic way were then asked to post in an **idealised** way, and vice versa.

[… We] discovered that after posting in an authentic way for a week, participants reported higher levels of **positive effect** and mood than they did after the week in which they posted to please others.

Source: *Scientific American*, 9 February 2021.

7   Read the extract from the article and then note down your responses to these questions:

a) What was the question the researchers were trying to answer?

b) Summarise their findings.

c) Do these research findings support the perspective given in the blog by Josh Renyard, or do they give a different perspective?

Final task

8   Create a blog post titled: 'How honest should we be when presenting ourselves online?' In the blog post:

a) Refer to the ideas you have read about and discussed, drawing on different perspectives.

b) Make it clear what your own opinion is, while also summarising the different conclusions other people have reached.

> ### Vocabulary
>
> **recruited**: got people to agree to do a certain job (here, answer research questions)
>
> **randomly**: by chance
>
> **assigned**: given the task of
>
> **authentic**: honest, genuine
>
> **idealised**: making something appear better than it is in reality
>
> **positive effect**: pleasant feelings brought about by everyday occurrences

? REFLECTION POINT

Why is it important to consider different perspectives? Why might considering a different perspective make you change your mind?

Did any of the perspectives you explored in this unit change your mind about how we should present ourselves online?

Studying an issue and its consequences on others

Skills focus
✓ Analysis
Learning focus
- Study a particular issue and suggest possible causes.
- Explain the consequences of an issue on other people.

Big question: What is the 'global village' – and is everyone part of it?

Getting started

Wai-Ling has taken up running. She needs ideas for music that will inspire her to keep going, even if the weather is poor and she's getting tired.

Wai-Ling decides to ask her friends for ideas, so she posts a request for suggestions on her social media account. She has friends all over the world and lots of them respond with great ideas for running music.

1 Working with a partner, discuss these ideas:

a) Why might posting a request online have been better than just asking friends who live nearby?

b) Why was Wai-Ling able to get so many responses?

Wai-Ling's mother said that she could never have done that when she was young. She would just have asked her friends in the street.

c) What are the causes of these changes?

d) What activities, other than listening to music, can be **enriched** by being connected to people in other parts of the world?

Exploring

The way that Wai-Ling uses her global connections means she is part of what is often called the 'global village'. This term, used since the 1960s, describes the world as a single community linked by **telecommunications**, in which distance is less significant and people are less isolated.

Since the invention of the internet in the 1990s, the global village has become more of a reality with the development of **digital communication systems**. Today, millions of people around the world can use their **smartphones** to record what is happening, rapidly sharing local events with people globally.

Vocabulary

enriched: improved in quality

telecommunications: communication using electronic means, for example radio, telephone, television and computer

digital communication systems: systems that share information using digital (numerical) signals

smartphone: mobile telephone with computer features, including email and internet access

bargain: negotiate to bring down the price of an item for sale

2 Working in a small group, read through this case study and the world facts. Then discuss and note down your responses to the questions that follow.

Mandev is a hill farmer in Nepal; he grows tomatoes. They sell for a good price at market; however, they are difficult to transport as they grow high up on the hillside. He loads them into baskets on donkeys to take to market.

Previously, he would do this hoping he could sell them all. However, sometimes when he arrived at the market, there would be several other tomato sellers there as well. Buyers could **bargain** and get the price down. Mandev would have to sell his tomatoes at a lower price or take them back home.

Today, Mandev uses his mobile phone to find out where the markets are, who else is at them, and how much tomatoes are selling for. This means he only goes to those markets where he can get a good price.

World facts

World population: 8.0 billion

Mobile phone owners: 7.3 billion

Smartphone owners: 6.5 billion

Internet users: 4.66 billion

Sources: data drawn from the United National Population Division; BankMyCell; FinancesOnline.

a) How has access to the global village changed the way that Mandev is working?

b) What are the consequences to Mandev of this?

c) Mandev upgrades his phone to a smartphone. How might this help him to improve his business further?

d) The internet speed in Mandev's village is slow. How might this affect his access to the global village?

e) Suggest barriers to accessing the global village that some people might experience.

Developing

Reema is writing an assignment on the consequences of the global village. Here are her notes.

- My country has access to communications technology we didn't have previously. The countries that developed this did so over many years and with huge investments.

- Electronic files – whether text, images, videos or music – can be shared widely and easily.

- Some people, and their ideas, can become very popular very quickly. Young people can be influenced by cultural ideas from other countries that undermine traditional values.

- Better communications can lead to **misinformation** such as fake news **circulating** easily.

- Powerful global companies can **exert** a powerful influence on people through their control of communication systems, such as **media outlets**.

Vocabulary

misinformation: false or inaccurate information, often spread deliberately

circulating: spreading throughout a system – here, global information systems

exert: to apply force

media outlets: forms through which news is published, such as television, radio, magazines and the internet

globalisation: the growth of interactions around the world between people, businesses and governments

3 Working in a small group, read through the points Reema has made.

a) For each point, consider how the impacts could be positive or negative.

Record your findings in a table like the one below. An example has been added, to start you off.

Impact of global village	Positive consequence	Negative consequence
Increased information sharing	Greater awareness of issues by a larger number of people	Spreading of misinformation

b) Are there any impacts of the global village that Reema hasn't thought of? Add these to your table.

Reema has done some secondary research to support her written assignment. She has noted down quotations from two sources.

Source A: From a blog post 'What is cultural **globalisation**?'
by Karl Thompson, 25 May 2017

[...]food consumption is an important aspect of culture and most societies around the world have diets that are unique to them[...] however the spread of global food corporations has arguably led to the decline of local diets and eating traditions.

Source B: From *Runaway World: How Globalisation is Shaping Our Lives* by Anthony Giddens, 2002.

We are the first **generation** to live in this society, whose **contours** we can as yet only dimly see. It is shaking up our existing ways of life, no matter where we happen to be. This is [...] not settled or secure, but **fraught** with anxieties, as well as scarred by deep divisions. Many of us feel in the grip of forces over which we have no power.

4 Working on your own, make notes in response to these questions:

a) Which points in Reema's notes does each source support?

b) Do you think these authors have a positive or a negative view of the impacts of the global village? Explain your answer.

c) Do you agree with the authors that being better connected to people throughout the world causes people to question their own way of life and traditions more?

d) For each source, identify two negative consequences of the global village. Refer to the case study on Mandev and the table from question 3 to help you.

Final task

5 Drawing on all the information in this unit, write an article of between 150 and 200 words summarising the idea of the global village and identifying its consequences for the world population.

Use the 'Checklist for success' to help you structure your article.

Checklist for success

✔ Explain clearly what the global village is.

✔ Explore the positive and negative consequences of the global village.

✔ Use information from the sources in this unit to support the points you make.

✔ Summarise your key points at the end.

❓ REFLECTION POINT

Think about your own personal experiences of the global village.

What have been the consequences of the global village for your country? Do you think overall that the global village has had a positive or a negative impact?

Suggesting different actions as responses to a global issue

Skills focus
✓ Analysis

Learning focus
- Identify and explore actions to address a national or global issue.
- Explore the implications of actions taken.
- Decide on a course of action following a consideration of alternatives.

Big question: Is learning better online or face to face?

Getting started

1 Working in a small group:

   a) Discuss your experiences of learning online. What do you like and dislike about it?

   b) Now discuss your experiences of learning face to face. What do you like and dislike about it?

   c) Together, create a grid showing the advantages and disadvantages of face-to-face and online learning. Does your group have a clear preference for one type of learning over the other?

Exploring

In 'Getting started', you discussed ideas about the big question: 'Is learning better online or face to face?' Now, you will explore the question in more depth, with a focus on two key areas:

- how easy it is to access teaching

- what enables students to learn more effectively.

These areas may require different actions in response to the question of what the role of online learning in education should be.

2 Read through the case study, then answer the questions that follow.

> ### Vocabulary
>
> **lecture**: an educational talk, often given to a large number of people
>
> **seminar**: discussion group led by a tutor
>
> **trial**: experiment in which you test something by using it or doing it for a set time
>
> **running costs**: money spent on the costs of using a building, for example heating, lighting, rent

---

Rahul is studying Law at university. He goes to **lectures** and **seminars**, where he discusses ideas with his tutors and peers. He learns how to argue and make a better case to convince other people.

The university then announces that it is going to **trial** online learning for the last six weeks of term. Students are sent home to complete their studies. Lectures are provided online; they are also recorded, allowing students to watch (and re-watch) them at any time.

Rahul appreciates being able to replay aspects of a lecture he finds difficult. Watching recordings also means he has been able to take on a part-time job in his local supermarket.

Rahul's tutor calls to discuss Rahul's progress. Rahul says he can follow the lectures but misses the interaction with the other students. When he attended lectures and seminars, he would talk about the ideas from the course – but that doesn't happen now. He can email questions to his tutor, but it takes time to get an answer, and he no longer enjoys lively discussions with his peers. He really misses that aspect of learning, which challenged him to improve his arguments.

Rahul's tutor sympathises, and reports that several of the students are feeling more isolated studying from home. However, she explains that it's much cheaper to run courses online. Many students are struggling to afford to pay the university fees, and the university's **running costs** have been going up. Rahul's tutor suggests that online learning will enable far more people to gain an education.

a) Working on your own, make some notes about the impact of the university moving its tuition online. Use a PMI grid like the one below to structure your ideas.

- Note down the advantages and disadvantages for the university and for students using the 'Plus' and 'Minus' columns.

- In the 'Interesting' column, note down any questions you have, or additional information you would like to find out.

	Plus	Minus	Interesting
University			
Students			

b) Put a ✓ next to any points that relate to how easy it is to access education.

c) Put a ✗ next to any points that relate to quality of education.

d) Share your ideas in a group. Note down any additional points from the discussion.

Developing

One of the recent growth areas in education has been Massive Open Online Courses (MOOCs). MOOCs are free web-based courses that large numbers of people can sign up for.

3 Read the two articles below, which give contrasting views of MOOCs. Then, work with a partner to answer these questions:

a) What do both articles agree on?

b) What does the author of the first article see as the key issue with MOOCs?

c) What evidence do they offer of this?

d) Why do the authors of the second article argue that MOOCs are making a useful difference?

e) What evidence do they offer of this?

f) Which arguments are focused on providing easier access to education? Which arguments are focused on what helps students to learn more effectively? Summarise these in a table.

Why MOOCs aren't working right now

by Harman Singh, CEO of Yuno Learning

Currently, just 10 per cent of MOOC **registrants** complete their courses. Why — if all the materials are free and available with the click of a mouse? MOOCs are structured using a series of pre-recorded video-based, self-paced classes offered to students for free. There are no live instructors to help **facilitate** the classes, lectures or content…and the format does not encourage the exchange of different thoughts and ideas among learners. The lack of live instructor involvement also means no follow-up with the student, or any assurance along the way that the student's learning **trajectory** is heading in the right direction. At the course's conclusion, only the learner can determine if he or she was successful.

The modern MOOC — without live and interactive teacher engagement — is essentially an internet version of a book.

Source: *Wired* magazine.

Vocabulary

registrants: those registered on a course

facilitate: support (a course of action)

trajectory: direction

Coursera: one of the main providers of online courses

credential: evidence of achievement, such as a certificate

absolute: total, complete

inception: starting point

tangible: definite; able to be seen physically

intangible: difficult to define or measure

prerequisites: required qualifications

socioeconomic status: a person's position in life based on their social class and financial situation

Who's benefiting from MOOCs, and why

by Chen Zhenghao and other authors

The critics are right that most people who start a MOOC don't finish: just 4 per cent of **Coursera** users who watch at least one course lecture go on to complete the course and receive a **credential**. However, given the large number of users involved, the **absolute** reach of MOOCs is still significant. For instance, more than one million people have completed a Coursera course since its **inception** in 2012, with over 2.1 million course completions as of April 2015…

The chart shows the breakdown of **tangible** and **intangible** education benefits from MOOCs.

The educational benefits of MOOCs

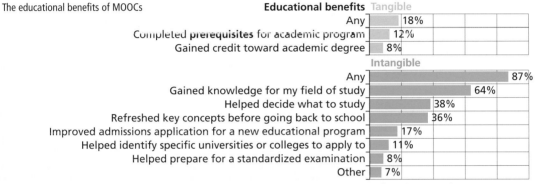

Educational benefits	Value
Tangible	
Any	18%
Completed **prerequisites** for academic program	12%
Gained credit toward academic degree	8%
Intangible	
Any	87%
Gained knowledge for my field of study	64%
Helped decide what to study	38%
Refreshed key concepts before going back to school	36%
Improved admissions application for a new educational program	17%
Helped identify specific universities or colleges to apply to	11%
Helped prepare for a standardized examination	8%
Other	7%

Source: *Harvard Business Review*/Coursera Survey Data.

…approximately half (47 per cent) of education seekers are students in a traditional academic setting. [Of these], 94% report some educational benefits from taking a MOOC.

Among the education seekers who are not in a traditional academic setting, disadvantaged populations are more likely to report educational benefits. Education seekers from developing countries [and] those with low **socioeconomic status** were more likely to report benefits than those with higher status.

Source: *Harvard Business Review*, 22 September 2015.

Final task

4 The university's trial of online learning is now over, and they are seeking feedback. You are asked to advise the university on whether it should switch completely to online learning.

Write at least two paragraphs summarising your recommendations.

- Draw on information in this unit, including your notes from earlier activities and the data in both articles.

- Consider the impact of online learning on access to education and quality of learning.

- If you think further information is needed before the university makes a final decision, state what else it should find out.

In this topic, you will be assessed on how well you can suggest and justify different actions to make a positive difference to a national or global issue.

❓ REFLECTION POINT

Do you think that online learning will play a significant role in improving the quality of education globally? What evidence would you offer to support your view?

Reflecting on the impact of exploring different perspectives

Skills focus
✓ Reflection

Learning focus
- State a personal perspective on a debateable issue.
- Consider alternative perspectives on a debatable issue.
- Reflect on whether considering other perspectives has changed your mind.

Big question: Is taking selfies selfish?

Getting started

1   The young person in this image is taking a **selfie** in a beautiful location – Mount Bromo, one of the most visited tourist attractions in Indonesia.

   a) What kind of location would you like to photograph yourself in?

   b) Why might a well-chosen selfie be something to **cherish**?

Exploring

Many people like to take pictures of themselves in different locations, to show their friends where they have been and what they have seen. This is nothing new – people have been taking photographs on holiday for years. Today, however, many people like to take a selfie using the camera on their phone and post it online.

Some tourist locations actively encourage people to take selfies while there – and it's easy to see why, as they provide the tourist spot with a form of free advertising. People seeing their friends in a beautiful and exciting location may decide they also want to go there. In this way, selfies have resulted in some tourist locations becoming far more popular.

2   With a partner, discuss the impacts on a local destination of tourists taking selfies there.

   a) What might the benefits of this be? Consider local and national consequences.

   b) Why might this start to cause problems for some popular tourist locations?

   c) Join together with another pair and discuss your responses. Do selfies taken in tourist locations bring mostly positive or negative impacts? Record your ideas in a table.

You are going to carry out a survey on attitudes towards tourists taking selfies, by using an opinion **continuum**.

Vocabulary

selfie: self-photograph taken on a smartphone, typically to be shared on social media

cherish: prize, value highly

selfie stick: metal rod designed to hold a mobile phone so that a person taking a selfie can do so from a greater distance

🔑 Key terms

continuum: line representing a continuous progression from one possibility to an opposing one

An example of an opinion continuum is shown below. One end of the continuum represents viewing something positively and the other end represents viewing something negatively. The example below shows an opinion continuum in relation to people's attitude towards cats, which runs from 1 ('I love cats') to 9 ('I dislike cats').

1	2	3	4	5	6	7	8	9
I love cats		I quite enjoy being around cats		I don't mind cats		I don't enjoy being around cats		I dislike cats

3

a) Where would you place yourself on the opinion continuum for cats? Choose a number, then share answers as a class.

b) Do you think the opinion continuum is a useful way of recording people's opinions? Why/why not?

4 Working on your own:

a) Create an opinion continuum about people taking selfies in tourist locations.

b) Decide where *you* stand on the continuum. Record this number and your reason why.

c) Find out from other people where they stand on the continuum and why. Decide on the best way to record your results.

d) Do you want to change your number on the continuum after speaking with other people?

e) Why do you think some people alter their opinion after listening to others?

Developing

Art galleries are another location where tourists like to take selfies.

5 If you were in an art gallery next to a famous painting, would you take a selfie? Why? Make notes to return to later.

Read this review comment from on an online tourist website. Another person has responded to the original post.

> **ArtFan** I'm fed up. I've just been to one of the bigger art galleries in Paris and it was packed with tourists with **selfie sticks**. Every time they got near a painting, they would turn their back on it, hold up the selfie stick and photograph themselves with the painting in the background. Some of them didn't even bother to look at the painting properly. Selfish behaviour, and a waste of their time and mine!

> **Mia T.** Quit complaining! Taking selfies is a great way of showing people where you've been. A person with a mobile phone doesn't take up any more space than someone without one!

6 If you were running an art gallery, what would you do in response to this feedback? Make notes to return to later.

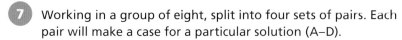

Following complaints from tourists about selfies ruining their enjoyment of art galleries, the gallery manager has proposed four solutions:

A: Continue with the gallery's current policy – all visitors can take photographs whenever they want.	B: **Ban** all visitors to the museum from taking photographs.
C: Introduce a 'photograph hour' at the start and end of each day; visitors will be **permitted** to take photographs only during these times.	D: Divide the area in front of each **exhibit**, so those taking photographs are kept to one side of a low **partition**.

7 Working in a group of eight, split into four sets of pairs. Each pair will make a case for a particular solution (A–D).

    a) In your pair, spend 5 minutes devising an argument to support your solution.

    b) Each group then has 2 minutes to explain and promote their solution.

8 Revisit your own point of view in light of the arguments you have just heard.

    a) Do you agree with any of the solutions A–D?

    b) Do you have an alternative solution – and, if so, what?

    c) Have your views in response to questions 3 and 4 changed as a result of hearing the different arguments?

> ### Vocabulary
>
> **ban**: prevent something from happening
>
> **permitted**: officially allowed
>
> **exhibit**: work of art on display in a museum, such as a painting or sculpture
>
> **partition**: division to separate parts or areas

Not only can taking selfies cause problems for other people, it can also be dangerous for the selfie taker, too. A report by the US National Library of Medicine in 2018 stated that 259 people died between October 2011 and November 2017 while taking selfies.

Many people have been injured while taking selfies. This includes a couple who were washed away by a giant wave, and a man who fell into a volcano and suffered burns. These people needed to be rescued by the emergency services.

In India, due to the increasing number of selfie deaths, the Ministry of Tourism asked states to identify 'selfie danger' areas and put safety barriers around them.

9 Revisit your work from question 2 on the impacts on a local destination of tourists taking selfies there. Update your table based on the information on the risks of taking selfies.

Final task

10 Return to your opinion continuum about people taking selfies in tourist locations.

a) Decide where you *now* stand on the continuum. Record this and your reason why.

b) Find out from other people who you interviewed earlier where they *now* stand on the continuum and their reason why.

c) Ask them to explain why their opinion has changed from earlier or has stayed the same.

d) Produce a summary report to share your findings. Think about:

- How will you show any key patterns, or **trends**, in the data?

- If people's opinions changed, how will you show what influenced them to change their opinion?

- If people's opinions were unchanged, how will you show their reasons?

End with a conclusion in which you summarise what your findings reveal about how considering other perspectives may influence people's opinions on a key issue. Include your own personal reflection on whether your opinion changed, and why.

> 🔑 **Key term**
>
> **trends**: patterns in data, in which the numbers change in a similar way

> ❓ **REFLECTION POINT**
>
> Why might it be a good thing to be influenced by alternative perspectives?
>
> Did the opinion continuum change the way you looked at selfies? Why?

Presenting evidence to support arguments

Skills focus
✓ Communication
Learning focus
- Present information in a clear and logical way.
- Offer explanations to support arguments made.
- Reference sources as appropriate.

Big question: Should we be excited or concerned by the 'internet of things'?

Getting started

People have been able to communicate with each other remotely for many years, but today, we can communicate with objects as well. For example, it is possible to adjust the heating and lighting in your home or change the music you are listening to, using voice command technology. You can access your smartphone using facial recognition technology. This ability to connect to everyday objects using the internet is known as the 'internet of things' (IoT).

1 Working in a group, share your experiences of the internet of things, or anything you have heard or read about this kind of technology.

Would you describe your experiences or the opinions of others about the internet of things as positive or negative? Why?

Exploring

Imagine you are out shopping. It's a warm day and you know your home will be hot when you return. Wouldn't it be good if you could open the air vents or even put the air-conditioning on before you get home? The internet of things means you can use your smartphone to do this.

In the future, the internet of things could mean that all the devices in your home have internet access. Not only would this enable you to control these devices remotely but it would also mean they could be programmed to interact with each other. For example, the airconditioner could be programmed to start cooling your home the moment you start the car or motorbike to come home.

2 Work in a group to design a poster to show what the home of the future, connected to the internet of things, might look like.

a) Decide among the group who will investigate which aspects of the future home. For example, you might choose to focus on lighting or temperature control, or how showers, washing machines or vacuum cleaners can be managed.

b) Each member of the group should research IoT technology linked to their chosen aspects of the home. Keep a record of the sources you gather information from.

c) Come back together as a group and plan how you will share your information with the class in a poster format.

You will need to decide as a group how you will organise the poster, what images you will include and how you will reference sources. For example, you could write these next to each item on the poster, or you could reference all sources together at the bottom of the page using a reference section. Use the 'Checklist for success' to help you.

Checklist for success

✔ The poster is clearly structured, well organised and visually appealing.

✔ The impact of technology on each aspect of the future home is summarised clearly and concisely.

✔ You have used images to support your explanation, where helpful.

✔ All sources used are clearly referenced.

---

3 Display your poster and look at those produced by other groups. See how information has been communicated in each poster.

a) Make notes on how well each poster has been done – including your group's – using the success criteria above.

b) Discuss your feedback as a class. Identify examples of what has been done well.

c) Could the information in your poster have been presented more clearly? Explain your thinking.

Developing

Does the internet of things sound too good to be true? Read these four opinions, which all consider problems linked to the IoT.

As electricity becomes more expensive and supplies less reliable, making our homes more dependent on electrical power is a crazy idea.

If a **hacker** gains access to just one of the connected devices in a home, they will be able to access everything – contact details, passwords, credit card numbers, security systems. It is estimated that criminals steal more than $1 trillion each year through online banking. Just think how bad it will be if our homes go 'online'.

The IoT is a rich person's dream. Everything in the IoT home, from light switches to heating control systems, will have to be replaced and then linked to a new interface unit. Most people globally simply can't afford it – 80 per cent of the world's population lives on less than $10 a day.

The more complex the system, the greater the chance that something will go wrong. What happens if all the appliances turn on and the security system **malfunctions**? Or you can no longer change the temperature of your shower **manually**?

Vocabulary

hacker: person who can use a computer to access data illegally

malfunctions: breaks down, goes wrong

manually: by hand

 4 a) Working with a partner, discuss and make notes on the strengths and weaknesses of each argument. Use the explanation on the right to help you.

b) Did any of these arguments convince you to change your opinion about the IoT? Why?

c) Feed back to the group. As a group, order the arguments from most to least convincing. Make sure you give clear reasons to support your decisions.

d) Discuss how each of the arguments could be stronger.

An argument is a point of view supported by evidence. A strong argument is one that offers more than one piece of evidence and even acknowledges opposing evidence.

Final task

Your school is thinking of investing in IoT technologies. You have been asked to carry out an analysis of the benefits and risks of doing so, and then present your recommendations.

5 Work in a group to carry out a risk–benefit analysis on the internet of things. You will need to draw on all your work from this unit and use this to produce a report.

a) Decide on four examples of IoT technologies that could be used in the school. You may need to do some research into these.

b) Explain what the internet of things is and how your four IoT technologies work. (You might want to include pictures to support your explanation.)

c) Outline the benefits to the school of each of your chosen IoT technologies. For example, how would they help the school to function more efficiently?

d) Explain the risks – or drawbacks – of your chosen IoT technologies. For example, if something went wrong, would they be expensive and difficult to repair?

e) Present your final recommendation on whether the school should invest in IoT technologies. You will need to reach a conclusion about whether the benefits of IoT technologies outweigh the risks, or whether the risks are too great.

Refer to the 'Checklist for success' to help you make your arguments convincing.

Checklist for success

✔ Present your argument in a clear and logical way.

✔ Use explanation to support the points you make.

✔ Draw on sources to support your arguments, where relevant.

> **? REFLECTION POINT**
>
> When you express a point of view, state why it is important to offer evidence.
>
> When you include evidence, explain why including a reference to the source is important.

Applying what you have learned

Your task

You are going to answer the question: 'Does the internet encourage us to live in 'bubbles'?'

A 'bubble' is a group of people who think about things in a similar way and share similar views. So, are people who use the internet more likely to communicate in 'bubbles' and less likely to explore and consider points of view other than their own?

To answer the question, you will need to carry out some primary research to ask people about:

- something they care about
- where they get their information from
- whether they listen to other points of view.

Approaching the task

It is easy to find other people that we agree with on the internet. We might do this by reading online articles or blogs, by watching videos or by joining communities on social media platforms. However, this can mean that we only interact with people who have a similar point of view, so we may never hear opposing arguments. Over time, this might make us more fixed in our views and less able to consider different perspectives.

You will need to carry out some interviews to explore this question. You don't need to interview a large group of people, but you do need to think carefully about the questions you will ask.

 Design a questionnaire that you can use. You will need to consider aspects such as:

- what people's key interests are
- who people interact with online to support these interests
- who people interact with offline to support these interests (for example, via local groups or magazines)

- how much these online and offline interactions support their interests; for example, you might ask how many times a day they look at a particular source

- the extent to which they interact with people with different – or opposing – views, both offline and online.

2 Decide on the people who you will interview. You should aim to interview at least four people.

3 Carry out the interviews. Make sure you record participants' responses in the same way.

4 When you have gathered your evidence, write a report on your findings. You will need to:

a) Summarise the issues that people said they care about and the sources of information they use to find out about these issues. This might include websites and social media, or newspapers and television channels. Think about a good way of showing this clearly.

b) Reach a conclusion about whether there is a **correlation** between the sources of information people use and how much they listen to opposing points of view. Do people who read newspapers, online or offline, consider opposing points of view more than those who spend more time on social media?

Use the 'Checklist for success' to help you write your report.

> **🔑 Key terms**
>
> **correlation**: relationship or connection between two or more things
>
> **inclined**: having a tendency towards something
>
> **empathise**: understand why someone thinks or feels something

---

Checklist for success

Your report should include the following.

✔ A clear written summary of what you learned by interviewing people.

✔ Well-structured conclusions with supporting evidence.

✔ Suggestions about whether some types of communication are better than others at encouraging consideration of different points of view.

✔ A conclusion about whether people are inclined to only share ideas with people with similar views.

Reflecting on your progress

Think back over this chapter. Give an example of:

- when you changed your point of view researching an issue

- when you had to understand and **empathise** with a point of view that wasn't yours

- a global issue that you had to suggest a suitable course of action on.

Suggest which of these three made the biggest impact on you and why.

Check your progress

Beginning	Developing	Going beyond
• I can consider a global or national issue and suggest a response.	• I can explore a global or national issue and suggest various responses.	• I can examine a global or national issue, suggest responses and evaluate them.
• I can suggest what might have caused something to happen and what might change as a result.	• I can suggest several possible causes of a situation and a few possible consequences of it.	• I can identify and evaluate a range of causes and consequences of a situation.
• I can look at some evidence and suggest a conclusion.	• I can analyse evidence and form a logical conclusion.	• I can analyse a range of evidence, form logical conclusions and suggest how confident I can be about them.
• I can suggest a good way of presenting information and state its source.	• I can present information clearly and reference sources.	• I can present a range of information clearly and reference various sources.

Next steps

Look at examples of how people, organisations and products are represented online. Reflect on decisions they have made about how they represent themselves. Decide what this suggests about them and their message.

Consider different ways of learning, both face to face and online, and work out which style of learning you prefer. Knowing how you learn effectively is an important skill.

Think about how you are influenced by ideas from other parts of the world compared with ideas from your own area or country.

When an issue is reported in the news, consider the causes and consequences of it. Sometimes reporters focus more on the immediate effects but try to take a longer view. If there are reports of flooding, for example, consider the possible causes and the longer-term consequences, too.

Bringing your skills together

What are the rights of a child?

7

In a century in which migration is an ever-growing issue, what rights does a child have wherever they come from and in whichever country they find themselves?

International problems need international solutions. However, different countries have different responses to migration and the law. How can we better understand these national perspectives, and make sure they are respected and represented when developing global law and policy?

In this chapter, you will be exploring the topics of 'Law and criminality' and 'Migration and urbanisation', thinking about the following issues:

- **How do we keep children safe when they move from one country to another?**

- **What is a national perspective on child migration?**

- **How do we reach an international agreement that reflects different national perspectives?**

- **How far can we achieve united agreement on solutions to a global issue?**

You will be revising and practising the analysis, evaluation, communication and reflection skills you have been developing across Stage 8:

7.1 Analysing and evaluating different national perspectives

7.2 Presenting an effective argument

7.3 Applying what you have learned: group activity

7.4 Applying what you have learned: individual report

7.5 Reflecting on what you have learned.

Your final task will be to write a personal reflection on what you have learned about the issue of child migration and the law, in which you demonstrate your understanding of different national perspectives on the topic.

Analysing and evaluating different national perspectives

Skills focus
✓ Analysis
✓ Evaluation
Learning focus
- Analyse the causes and consequences of a global issue.
- Evaluate different sources, analysing the same issue from different national perspectives.
- Recognise bias in a source and assess its credibility.

Big question: How do we keep children safe when they move from one country to another?

Getting started

The international rights of all children are set out in the United Nations Convention of the Rights of the Child (UNCRC). This is legally binding on all but one of its member states.

There are 54 articles in the UNCRC, which include rights to:

- life, survival and development

- protection from violence, abuse or neglect

- an education that enables children to fulfil their potential

- a parental relationship

- express their opinions and be listened to.

The world's first declaration on children's rights was written by Eglantyne Jebb, the founder of Save the Children, in 1923. You can find out more about the rights of children, including a young-person friendly version of the UNCRC, on the Save the Children website.

1 Working in a group, answer the following questions:

   a) What are your basic rights at home and at school?

   b) How does your country and your school protect those rights?

   c) How do you know what you are and are not allowed to do?

   d) How are you kept safe from criminal behaviour?

   Share your responses with the rest of the class.

Exploring

When you move country, you move to a different legal system. If a young person's migration is not legal, or they and their parents do not have the correct paperwork, they can struggle to establish their rights or to have the protection of the law. This means that children can be **detained** and treated as criminals.

The following article from a news website considers the problems **refugee** and **migrant** children face in meeting their basic needs.

> **Vocabulary**
>
> **detained**: held in a type of prison (detention centre)
>
> **refugee**: person who has had to leave their country of origin because they are in danger; refugees have a right to international protection
>
> **migrant**: person who has chosen to live outside their country of origin

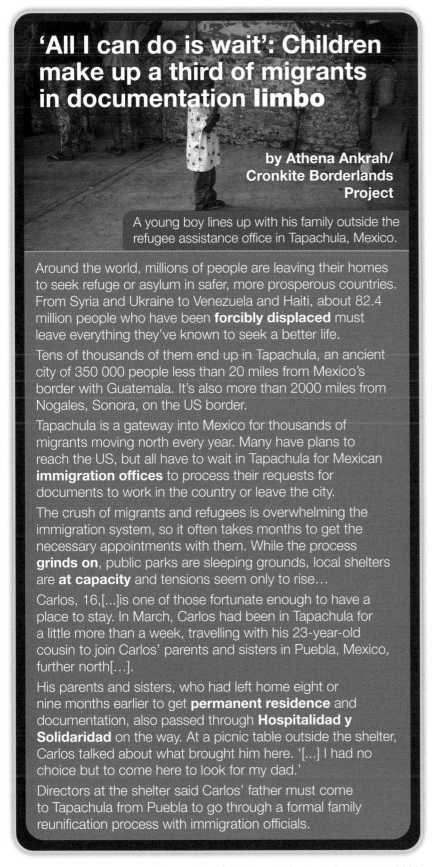

'All I can do is wait': Children make up a third of migrants in documentation **limbo**

by Athena Ankrah/ Cronkite Borderlands Project

A young boy lines up with his family outside the refugee assistance office in Tapachula, Mexico.

Around the world, millions of people are leaving their homes to seek refuge or asylum in safer, more prosperous countries. From Syria and Ukraine to Venezuela and Haiti, about 82.4 million people who have been **forcibly displaced** must leave everything they've known to seek a better life.

Tens of thousands of them end up in Tapachula, an ancient city of 350 000 people less than 20 miles from Mexico's border with Guatemala. It's also more than 2000 miles from Nogales, Sonora, on the US border.

Tapachula is a gateway into Mexico for thousands of migrants moving north every year. Many have plans to reach the US, but all have to wait in Tapachula for Mexican **immigration offices** to process their requests for documents to work in the country or leave the city.

The crush of migrants and refugees is overwhelming the immigration system, so it often takes months to get the necessary appointments with them. While the process **grinds on**, public parks are sleeping grounds, local shelters are **at capacity** and tensions seem only to rise…

Carlos, 16,[…]is one of those fortunate enough to have a place to stay. In March, Carlos had been in Tapachula for a little more than a week, travelling with his 23-year-old cousin to join Carlos' parents and sisters in Puebla, Mexico, further north[…].

His parents and sisters, who had left home eight or nine months earlier to get **permanent residence** and documentation, also passed through **Hospitalidad y Solidaridad** on the way. At a picnic table outside the shelter, Carlos talked about what brought him here. '[…] I had no choice but to come here to look for my dad.'

Directors at the shelter said Carlos' father must come to Tapachula from Puebla to go through a formal family reunification process with immigration officials.

Source: *Cronkite News*, Arizona PBS, 1 August 2022.

Vocabulary

limbo: situation of uncertainty while awaiting a decision

forcibly displaced: made to leave their country for reasons beyond their control

immigration offices: places that deal formally with people who are new arrivals in a different country

grinds on: continues, but at a very slow pace

at capacity: full, with no available space

permanent residence: the right to remain in a country

Hospitalidad y Solidaridad: charity offering shelter and support

2 Read the article on page 129, then discuss these questions with a partner:

   a) How does the article set out a global problem?

   b) Why is there a specific national problem?

   c) Why is this a matter of the law?

   d) What local problems has this caused for the city of Tapachula?

   e) What is the local solution?

   f) How does this article relate to the rights of the child?

The following article about child migration is from the website of UNICEF, the United Nations Children's Fund.

Vocabulary

persistent: continual, recurring again and again

protracted: over a long period of time

compounded: made worse

shuttered: closed down

complement: go along with

amplified: supported or reinforced

Solar-powered radios are helping conflict-affected and displaced children follow lessons outside of the classroom

By Fatou Diagne

SÉGOU REGION, Mali – **Persistent** insecurity in central and northern Mali has helped fuel a **protracted** humanitarian crisis, disrupting access to education, health and other services, and displacing more than 300,000 people – more than half of them children.

COVID-19 has **compounded** the problem. Before the pandemic, direct threats and attacks on education had forced the closure of around 1,300 schools in central and northern regions. But pandemic-related measures **shuttered** schools across the country for most of 2020, leaving many of the most vulnerable young people unable to access education.

UNICEF has been distributing solar-powered radios in conflict-affected areas to vulnerable households and listening groups, where as many as 15 young people can make use of the same radio. The devices provide an educational lifeline for those who might otherwise be cut off from classes and **complement** the efforts of temporary learning spaces that have been established at sites for internally displaced persons to ensure that children can continue to learn in safety.

Aichata, 15, used to attend school in Diabaly, a rural town in the south-central region of Ségou. A few months after Aichata's school closed, her father decided the family should move to the town of Ségou, where she was enrolled at the Adama Dagnon school. The school provided her with a solar-powered radio to allow her to continue learning out of hours and make up for lost time. 'I could attend classes with this radio. It helped me catch up with my studies,' she says. [...]

'Before, I didn't like grammar because I didn't understand it and I found it difficult. But now I manage to get quite good marks,' she says. 'One time I got 8 out of 10 – I was really proud of myself!' [...]

In the Ségou region alone, around 1,500 households have benefited from the solar-powered radios. These efforts are being **amplified** by listening groups supported by a community relay, typically a retired teacher, who can help keep students' learning on track. [...]

Aichata hopes to eventually become a school principal so that she can help other children attend school. 'I know it's ambitious to say that every child in Mali will go to school,' she says. 'But I'm sure that one day my dream will come true.'

Source: UNICEF

UNICEF has a six-point Agenda for Action for Refugee and Migrant Children, which can be summarised as follows:

End the **detention** of refugee and migrant children		Keep families together to protect children's legal status
Protect children from **exploitation** and violence	**UNICEF's six-point Agenda for Action**	Keep refugee and migrant children learning
Press for action on the underlying causes of large-scale movement of refugees and migrants		Campaign for legal protection against discrimination in countries that children move through and end up in

3

a) Working with a partner, discuss and consider how these six points are relevant to the lives of Aichata and Carlos.

b) Feed back to the rest of the class about the six points and the issues these children face.

4 Working on your own, answer the following questions, which compare the two articles.

a) One article is from a news source, and the other is a page from an international organisation's website. Does that make a difference to their **credibility**?

b) What is the **campaigning focus** of the second article?

c) Why do both articles focus on the story of a single individual?

d) How do both sources put these stories into a global context?

e) What are the specific national issues in each case?

f) What overall **principles**, enforced in law, could make life easier for both children?

Developing

Keeping families together is one of UNICEF's Agenda for Action points, but another is education. This is an area where refugee and migrant children often miss out, whatever the reason they have moved. This is true even when they are internal migrants, moving within the same country. You can research this on the Save the Children website.

In South America, for example, one country's economic success made it an attractive 'host' country for many refugees and migrants, especially during the pandemic, but this has made it hard for the country to fulfil the educational needs of the children arriving. One study gives the following barriers to education faced by refugee and migrant children:

- insufficient space available (45 per cent)

- lack of access to the internet to **enrol** (29 per cent)

- arrival after enrolment had closed (23 per cent) (Save the Children).

Vocabulary

detention: imprisonment or confinement

exploitation: being put to work unfairly in order to benefit others

campaigning focus: the issue the article wants to highlight

principles: a fundamental truth which everyone can agree is important

enrol: officially register for a course or education setting

Key term

credibility: the extent to which something can be trusted and is believable

The research also revealed that over a quarter of migrant children who were enrolled in schools did not attend classes daily. This was due to limited access to the technology needed to attend remote classes, and the need to combine schooling with household chores, including caring for other children.

5 Discuss your answers to these questions with a partner, then share your ideas with the class.

a) What kind of research forms the basis of this information?

b) Which of the six principles in UNICEF's Agenda for Action are being ignored here?

c) Give three reasons why migrant and refugee children are not attending school in the host country.

Refugee and migrant children can also face prejudice and discrimination in host countries; some examples of this are given below.

> Are these really refugees or economic migrants?

> How can we be sure these are children if they don't have proper paperwork?

> A lot of these people are brought in by criminal gangs, and then our country pays for them to stay in three-star hotels.

6 Discuss in your group:

a) the credibility of these claims

b) whether people in countries you know agree or disagree with these viewpoints

c) why these views might prevent children's legal rights to family and education becoming a national priority.

Share your views with the rest of the class.

The protection of migrant and refugee children is clearly a global problem, but one on which there are many different and sometimes conflicting national perspectives. In the UK, for example, while some people share the prejudices expressed in the speech bubbles above, many cities have joined the City of Sanctuary scheme to demonstrate their support for migrants and refugees. However, an issue with international causes will also require international solutions.

National law is made by individual countries. International organisations such as the EU and UN can enforce compliance through international courts.

Final task

Your teacher will hand each pair of students a card with the name of a different country. You will continue to represent this country for the remaining group activities in this chapter.

7 With a partner, research how migration and asylum-seeking have affected the country you have been given. Search their current situation in an online encyclopaedia. Is your country one that many wish to leave or which many wish to come to? Find out what you can about your country from reliable sources and news media on the internet.

Answer the following questions as part of your research:

a) What is the biggest migration problem that your given country has?

b) Is it a 'host country' or one that many people wish to leave?

c) What are the causes and consequences of this?

d) What problems does this cause for children?

e) What is the government's attitude towards refugees and migrants?

f) What is their attitude towards international law?

g) What difficulties do they face in finding solutions to these issues without help from other countries?

8 Present the national perspective of 'your' country to the rest of the class. Remember that you need to support your viewpoint with evidence (information) and reasoning (appreciation of why your country thinks the way it does).

Different perspectives will lead to different views. The credibility of a viewpoint depends on how well it is supported by evidence, its lack of bias and the national or international perspectives that it represents.

? REFLECTION POINT

Based on your work in this unit, consider your views in response to the following questions:

- How do national perspectives differ from purely local perspectives?

- How do different cultures influence a national perspective on a global issue?

Try to come up with examples to support your understanding of different perspectives.

Presenting an effective argument

Skills focus
✓ Evaluation
✓ Communication
Learning focus
- Discuss the effectiveness of a single, complex argument.
- Make explicit reference to its structure and use of evidence.
- Present clearly reasoned and referenced arguments.

Big question: How do we reach an international agreement that reflects different national perspectives?

Getting started

At Stage 8, Global Perspectives involves researching national solutions to global problems.

The United Nations (UN) is a forum where different nations are represented and try to work together to make global statements based on international law, such as the UN Convention on the Rights of the Child.

The UN General Assembly Hall where all 193 member states are represented.

1 Working with a partner, discuss your responses to these questions:

   a) What global issues do you think are debated currently in the United Nations?

   b) What kind of concerns do you think your given country has raised at the United Nations?

Exploring

The following blog is by a **policy adviser** at UNICEF UK, the UN's agency to provide aid for children. It was written for COP25, the UN Climate Change conference in 2019, and addresses the issue of migration because of climate change.

2 Read the extract from the blog, then discuss these questions with a partner.

   a) Do you agree with the overall direction of the writer's argument?

   b) How has the writer structured their argument?

   c) What evidence do they use to support it?

   d) Which specific countries do they reference in their evidence?

www.Climate…

Climate migration and education: are we making our education systems future-proof?

by Anja Nielsen, 2 December 2019

What is climate migration – and why does education matter?

The International Organisation for Migration has defined environmental migrants as 'persons or groups of persons who, for **compelling** reasons of sudden or **progressive** changes in the environment that **adversely** affect their lives or living conditions, are obliged to leave their homes or choose to do so, either temporarily or permanently, and who move either within their country or abroad.'[1] Estimates of the number of environmental migrants by 2050 range from 25 million to 1 billion.[2] A 2018 report from the World Bank found that, in just three regions, over 140 million people could be forced to move due to 'the slow-**onset** impacts of climate change'.[3] It is clear that climate change will have a big impact on migration – and schools play a key role in securing children's rights throughout the process.

Children on the move face challenges in accessing education

Children on the move face multiple challenges to accessing and thriving in education. UNHCR notes that there are 3.7 million refugee children out of school, with 76 per cent of all secondary school-aged refugees not enrolled in education.[4] **Systemic**, social, legal and economic barriers all present themselves as displaced children seek to access education. For example, being taught in a non-native language, missing legal documentation required for school registration, or financial barriers can all keep children on the move out of education. Many of these challenges are directly referenced in UNICEF's six-point Agenda for Action for Refugee and Migrant Children[5], as well as in other international efforts to support children on the move. These will become more necessary than ever as climate change affects migration.

Support is needed before and after migration

…Before the move, education systems can reduce the impact of climate change on migration through Disaster Risk Reduction (DRR) – promoting **resilience** to disasters through teaching, infrastructure and safe school environments.[6] While DRR can help prevent some migration, not all movement can be avoided. In these cases, education sectors can **impart** the transformative and **transferable** skills that children need to succeed in their new communities. This can include ensuring that qualifications are recognised across borders.

Vocabulary

policy adviser: person who researches and analyses policies in a chosen area of study and then makes recommendations regarding them

compelling: persuasive, convincing

progressive: happening gradually in stages

adversely: negatively

onset: the beginning of something

systemic: based on ways that systems are set up

resilience: the ability to cope well with difficult circumstances

impart: to pass on, make known

transferable: able to be used in different situations

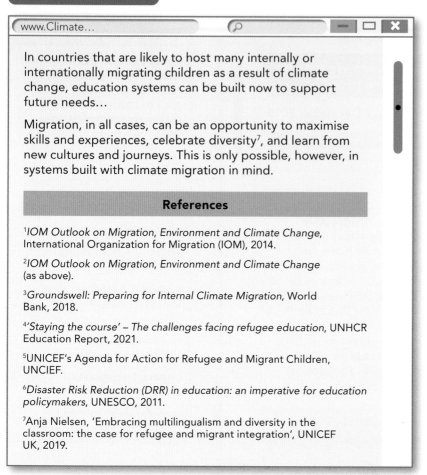

In countries that are likely to host many internally or internationally migrating children as a result of climate change, education systems can be built now to support future needs…

Migration, in all cases, can be an opportunity to maximise skills and experiences, celebrate diversity[7], and learn from new cultures and journeys. This is only possible, however, in systems built with climate migration in mind.

References

[1]*IOM Outlook on Migration, Environment and Climate Change,* International Organization for Migration (IOM), 2014.

[2]*IOM Outlook on Migration, Environment and Climate Change* (as above).

[3]*Groundswell: Preparing for Internal Climate Migration,* World Bank, 2018.

[4]*'Staying the course' – The challenges facing refugee education,* UNHCR Education Report, 2021.

[5]UNICEF's Agenda for Action for Refugee and Migrant Children, UNCIEF.

[6]*Disaster Risk Reduction (DRR) in education: an imperative for education policymakers,* UNESCO, 2011.

[7]Anja Nielsen, 'Embracing multilingualism and diversity in the classroom: the case for refugee and migrant integration', UNICEF UK, 2019.

Source: UKFIET.

Referencing sources used

In the blog, references were given in the form of **hyperlinks** to websites and publications. This is one way in which you can provide references **embedded** within an argument. The blog was also published on UNICEF UK's website; it was referenced to the original on the UKFIET website through a hyperlink: https://www.ukfiet.org/2019/climate-migration-and-education-are-we-making-our-education-systems-future-proof/.

Other ways of referencing are:

- Harvard referencing – quoting the author's name and year of publication within the article, for example Nielsen (2019), followed by the date when you accessed and checked the link

- footnoting – using **superscript** numbers within the article to link to a numbered list of sources at the end of the article. This is the system of referencing that has been used in the blog above.

You should follow referencing within your argument with a **bibliography** of sources, sometimes with a brief evaluation of and comment on each source.

> ### 🔑 Key terms
>
> **hyperlink**: electronic link that takes you to another website or online article
>
> **embedded**: set within
>
> **superscript**: when a number or letter is raised above the text line, usually in a smaller font, like this [1]
>
> **bibliography**: list of books or articles referenced

3 Now, working on your own, answer the following questions to evaluate the effectiveness of this argument based on its structure and use of evidence.

a) What is the writer's source for the definition of a 'climate change migrant'?

b) Why are statistics an important element of their argument?

c) What is especially shocking about the statistics concerning the education of migrant children?

d) Which three things especially keep migrant children out of education?

e) Where does the evidence the writer uses come from?

f) What are the strengths and weaknesses of their use of international sources?

g) Which actions does the writer recommend to reduce climate change migration?

h) Which actions do they recommend to host countries in order to prepare for climate change migration?

i) Are these actions clear, specific and evidence-based?

When your teacher has looked at your responses, discuss the answers with the rest of the class.

Developing

So, what makes an effective argument in an international forum? As we have seen, effective arguments:

- need to be fact-based

- respond to a current situation or crisis

- draw on reliable sources of evidence

- make clear recommendations for action.

The UN is a forum for different nations to discuss global issues and make and agree resolutions that propose action. So, it attempts to find international solutions to global issues, but it also represents different national interests and perspectives. This is achieved in the form of **resolutions**. Each resolution has two parts:

- First, there are **pre-ambulatory clauses**, which present the history of an identified issue with reference to particular countries and current problems.

- Then come **operative clauses**, which present a solution.

Normally, the UN tries to proceed with **consensus**, so the resolution should present as many perspectives as possible and reach agreement on global actions.

> **🔑 Key terms**
>
> **resolution**: firm decision about how to act
>
> **pre-ambulatory clause:** part of the resolution that explains the causes, consequences and context of the issue
>
> **operative clause:** part of the resolution that suggests specific actions, whether national or international
>
> **consensus**: agreement

Many schools have Model United Nations (MUN) clubs and attend or even host MUN conferences, where students organised in national teams represent different countries and take part in a mock United Nations debate, both in committee (smaller groups of countries) and General Assembly (all nations).

The UN debates a UN report on children and armed conflict, July 2018.

4 With your country partner, carry out internet research into the UN and Model United Nations. Look at the official UN website. You will also find support online, especially about how countries write resolutions and contribute to debate.

Answer these questions about UN debate, which will also help you organise a MUN conference.

a) What are the key committees of the UN?

b) What kind of issues do they debate?

c) What is a resolution?

d) Who writes and proposes a resolution?

e) How is a resolution structured?

f) Who decides if a resolution is adopted for debate?

g) What is the purpose of debate on a resolution?

h) If adopted, what happens to a resolution next?

Final task

5 You are the representatives of the country you were allocated in Unit 7.1, and you are sitting on a UN committee that will agree on further progress in protecting the rights of migrant and refugee children.

Working with a partner and using the research you did in the previous unit, draft a UN resolution presenting your national perspective but with the aim of achieving the agreement of other countries. You want your resolution to be debated and adopted!

a) Make it clear which committee your resolution is intended for and what question you are addressing using a brief title such as 'The question of child refugees and migrants'.

b) Write the resolution as one that your committee could take to General Assembly. Just as in Global Perspectives work, you need to address a focused question, although here you are phrasing the resolution as an answer, for example, 'The question of the rights of child refugees and migrants in South America'.

c) You will need about 6–10 'pre-ambulatory clauses'. They need to:

- give context to the resolution

- be based on recent events that indicate the need for more action

- describe the causes and the consequences of the current issue

- be fact-based

- express the concerns from your national perspective.

These will be discussed and amended in committee.

d) The 'operative clauses' then follow; these are recommendations for action. Each action point needs to be specific (remember what you have learned about **SMART** targets). These are things you request, recommend, urge or encourage countries to do.

Use the 'Checklist for success' to help you present clearly reasoned and referenced arguments.

> ## Key term
>
> **SMART**: Specific, Measurable, Attainable, Realistic, Time-bound

Checklist for success

✔ Do your arguments link to evidence and recent events?

✔ Are they structured and reasoned, addressing causes, consequences and solutions?

✔ Have you supported your viewpoint with references to studies and factual information?

? REFLECTION POINT

Now that you have written a draft resolution, reflect on how well it persuaded others to agree with your perspective.

Did you represent your national perspective on the global issue in a way that will win agreement from other countries?

Language support

Pre-ambulatory clauses start with words like 'observing', 'noting that', 'concerned by' or 'acknowledging'.

Each operative clause must begin with a verb because these are recommendations for action. The language you use should be formal and polite, for example 'requests', not 'demands', 'agrees' or 'suggests' rather than 'urges'.

Applying what you have learned: group activity

Skills focus
✓ Communication

Learning focus
- Select relevant information and arguments.
- Present reasoning based on evidence, referencing sources where appropriate.
- Use primary and secondary research to justify your goal.

Your task

Working as a group in three committees, pairs from different countries will finalise their resolutions from Unit 7.2 for presentation to the Model United Nations (MUN) General Assembly. The best of these resolutions will go forward for the MUN General Assembly debate. The aim is to reach broad agreement on international actions that support national solutions to the global issue of the legal rights of child refugees and migrants.

Approaching the task: UN committees

For this task, you will continue to represent the same country (you could use the flag of that country to show this). However, for your resolution to move forward for debate, you need co-signatories. The more countries you can persuade to support your resolution, the more likely it is to be adopted. This discussion takes place in committees. Once a resolution has been passed by the committee, it can progress to the General Assembly.

The actual United Nations has six committees.

First Committee (**Disarmament** and International Security)

Second Committee (Economic and Financial)

Third Committee (Social, Humanitarian and Cultural)

Fourth Committee (Special Political and **Decolonisation**)

UN committees

Fifth Committee (**Administrative** and Budgetary)

Sixth Committee (Legal)

1. Working with your country partner (Unit 7.2), research the six committees. Find out what they debate and how they call witnesses before finalising resolutions.

2. Which three committees would be most likely to discuss the legal rights of child refugees and migrants? Discuss this question with your partner and then with your teacher.

You might consider:

- How international security is threatened by uncontrolled migration
- Lack of education for refugee and migrant children
- How human rights are denied when refugee and migrant children are detained
- The legal framework set out in the UN Convention of the Rights of the Child, which UN member states have signed up to comply with.

Vocabulary

disarmament: reducing armaments (military weapons and equipment)

decolonisation: the process of ensuring that nations can control their own affairs, having previously been controlled by other countries

administrative: relating to the processes involved in running a business or organisation

Your teacher will:

- allocate each representative of your country to two of three committees

- allocate a Chair to each committee, whose role will be to act with neutrality and ensure the committee reaches an agreement, and work with the Vice-Chair

- allocate a Vice-Chair to each committee, to help pairs of countries improve their draft resolutions.

You will take your draft resolution to the committee. It is the purpose of the committee:

- to obtain signatories for a single resolution that commands a large amount of agreement as the best one to put forward to the General Assembly

- to evaluate both the pre-ambulatory and operative clauses

- to debate and, if necessary, amend the resolution so that it represents the views of the committee.

Remember that committees generally work by consensus, so you want to achieve agreement with the other members – but, if necessary, you can decide by majority vote.

Approaching the task: debate in committee

Your committee will need to evaluate the relative strengths of each resolution which its members have prepared and decide which is the best resolution to put forward.

3 You will now work with a different partner, representing a different country and a different national perspective.

Together, you will examine the strengths of the arguments that make up your countries' 'pre-ambulatory clauses'.

a) Explore the reasons and evidence used to support the pre-ambulatory clauses.

- Is the claim about the need for action suitably supported?

- How strong are the reasons? How factually based is the evidence?

- Is the past history (the claims or context) of the issue clearly represented?

b) Evaluate each other's resolutions and decide which is the best to co-sign. You can always propose clauses from the 'losing' resolution as potential amendments in committee.

4 **a)** As a pair of countries, examine the 'operative clauses', or recommendations for action.

- How well-supported are these by evidence?

- Are the clauses well-worded and reasoned?

- Do they move from immediate action towards future recommendations?

- Are the goals SMART? (In particular, they should be specific and achievable.)

b) Which operative clauses will you co-sign? You can amend a joint resolution made up of the best parts of each team's resolution, but you will need to make sure it has a consistent perspective on the issue.

5 Give your draft resolution to the Chair and Vice-Chair. They will now decide on the resolution you will debate as a committee. You need to accept the Chair's decision as final.

6 Now debate the chosen resolution in your committee. Remember that when you speak to the committee, you are the **delegate** of your country, so you need to represent their national perspective. However, the resolution also needs to represent the global perspective of your committee.

- If you represent the country that submitted the resolution, you should propose it.

- If you have concerns about any clauses in the resolution, you can propose amending them, deleting them or replacing them with clauses of your own.

Remember to:

☐ Be polite – show the other delegates respect. Do not talk over each other.

☐ Always address the Chair of the committee.

☐ Do not refer to other delegates by name, but as 'the delegate for [country]'.

The committee should try to reach consensus, but you can have a vote if necessary. The Chair will decide on this and guide discussion throughout. Amendments can also be voted on.

> ### Vocabulary
>
> **delegate**: a person who represents others, either an elected or appointed representative

Approaching the task: debate in General Assembly

Once the three committees have considered their resolutions, they can be discussed in General Assembly. There should be three different perspectives on the issue:

* International security

* Economic and financial welfare

* Human rights.

It is the role of the General Assembly to consider and balance out these different perspectives. It then creates a composite resolution that:

* brings together the best elements of all three resolutions

* presents a consistent perspective based on evidence and reasoning

* recommends a course of action that will be acceptable to all nations

* results in broad agreement.

7 General Assembly debating is fun, but it might be best chaired by your teacher. As a whole class, you will go through the same process as with the committees.

a) Decide which resolution commands most support.

b) Debate the resolution, aiming to call on as many countries to speak as possible.

c) Vote on amendments, deletions and changes to the resolution.

d) Reach agreement on the resolution to adopt. Any country can call for a vote.

Checklist for success

✔ Are you able to represent your national perspective?

✔ Does the resolution represent all global perspectives?

✔ Are your arguments well-structured and based on reasoning and evidence?

✔ Do the operative clauses represent a clear call for action?

✔ Do you listen to and respond to ideas and information from others?

✔ Do your contributions move the discussion on and show understanding of the issue?

Reflecting on your progress

How happy were you with the final resolution? Did it suggest a clear action that could be adopted by your nation?

How skilled are you in communicating information and arguments, and listening and responding?

Has debate helped you to understand different perspectives on the global issue of the rights of refugee and migrant children?

Applying what you have learned: individual report

Skills focus
✓ Communication
Learning focus
- Present information and arguments clearly.
- Provide written reasoning to support your arguments, referencing sources.

Your task

You will work on your own for this task. As Ambassador to the United Nations from your country, you will write a report on the global problem of child migration and the law. You will detail your national perspective, the UN debate, similarities and differences between the national views presented, and your recommendation for one national action. Your report will be 500–600 words.

Approaching the task: Structuring the report

A guide for structuring the report is given below. You can use the headings provided or your own. Word limits are suggested. Your teacher can look at your work in draft and give general feedback on progress to the whole class but won't assess your work until it is complete. The work must be entirely your own.

Issue and question (25 words)	• Identify the issue clearly. • Put together a research question: find a question that your report will be designed to answer.
Global and national perspectives (50–100 words)	• Identify both a global and a national perspective on this issue. The global perspective should have been set out by the MUN debate in Unit 7.3. In the final task for Unit 7.1, your pair discovered your country's national perspective on the issue. • State whether the global and national perspectives are similar or different.
Your research (250–300 words)	• Summarise your research and that of your classmates in the operative clauses of the MUN resolutions. • Set out the context and current issues debated. Make sure you cover the causes and consequences of current problems.

Your recommendation (100 words)	There are two parts to this:
	1. Set out the General Assembly recommendations that emerged from the MUN debate in Unit 7.3. Use the operative clauses of the final resolution and the drafts you discussed.
	2. Set out one national action – a law for your nation – which helps resolve the issue.
	Remember, your final recommendation needs to follow the UN resolution *and* respect your national perspective. Otherwise, it is unlikely to succeed – and you are unlikely to remain the Ambassador!
Evaluation of sources (75 words)	Set out the sources of information used and – in one sentence – summarise the credibility of their argument.

Use the 'Checklist for success' to make your own assessment of your report.

Checklist for success

✔ The research question is clear and focuses on the issue.

✔ Global and national perspectives are presented convincingly.

✔ Explanation is given of the similarities and differences between global and national perspectives.

✔ The research analyses the issue in detail and identifies clear and relevant causes and consequences.

✔ A realistic national course of action (a law) is clearly set out and explained.

✔ Two or three sources of information are clearly identified and evaluated.

✔ The report is structured well and easy to follow.

What is your teacher looking for?

Your teacher will be assessing your communication skills through the way you present: the issue, different perspectives, your research, a recommended course of action.

Reflecting on your progress

Use a traffic light (Red, Amber, Green) rating for each of these questions:

• How confident are you in writing up Global Perspectives activities?

• Have you found it easy to structure your report and organise your time?

• How comfortable are you with the language of Global Perspectives?

• How helpful did you find input from others during the debate?

• How confident are you in your own research and ideas?

Reflecting on what you have learned

Skills focus
✓ Reflection
Learning focus
* Identify the skills you have learned or improved on.
* Relate these to your own personal strengths and weaknesses.
* Work out which skills you most need to improve.

Your task

For this task, you will write an individual personal reflection of up to 500 words on what you have learned in this assessment chapter.

Approaching the task

The purpose of this assessment chapter has been to:

* develop your confidence in exploring global issues, researching different national perspectives, and proposing a national action as part of the solution

* revisit how you evaluate the credibility and bias of different sources

* synthesise different national perspectives on an issue so as to present an international viewpoint based on evidence and reasoning.

In the research report in Unit 7.4, you wrote up what you and the other groups discovered about the issue of the legal rights of refugee and migrant children and proposed one course of action – a law – for the nation you had studied, in response to the MUN resolution you debated.

In Global Perspectives, you conclude an individual research report with a personal reflection: you explore and evaluate how your research has changed your own personal reflection on the issue.

At the end of Student Book 7, you wrote an individual reflection on a group task. This helped you to understand that in Global Perspectives while you often work in a team, you learn as an individual. In Unit 7.4, you put together an individual, research-based report on a significant global issue, presenting a national perspective and solution. This is the kind of task you will need to do for the Cambridge Lower Secondary Checkpoint assessment at the end of Stage 9, where you choose your topic and devise your own research question.

In Global Perspectives, there are two types of reflection:

- Reflecting on your thoughts and actions in response to an issue
- Reflecting on the skills you have demonstrated.

Planning the task

For the conclusion of the report, you need to focus on the first kind of reflection. Use this table to plan your reflection.

1. Your initial perspective on the issue	Before you started your research, what did you know and think about the rights of children, especially migrants and refugees?
2. Your developing perspective on the issue	How has your thinking about this issue changed or developed as a result of what you have read, heard or done?
3. The link between what you have researched and what you now think	Be clear about exactly what has changed your mind or developed your ideas.
4. What did you understand about global and national perspectives on the issue?	Explain what you knew about your own country and its attitude to refugee and migrant children and their rights.
5. How has your understanding of global and national perspectives developed?	How did the MUN debate and your preparation for it make you more aware of different national perspectives and the difficulties of reaching international agreement?
6. Why different perspectives matter	Explore what makes this a global issue and why understanding different national perspectives can change attitudes and behaviour.
7. End with own personal perspective	Always end with your own personal perspective: what has changed in your understanding of the issue and how this will affect what you will think and do in the future.

Language support

Reflection is thinking about what you do and how you do it in a way that helps you make progress.

1 **a)** Write a personal reflection on what you have learned from the individual task in this unit.

- You can write up to 200 words.

- Your teacher may give you general advice on drafts, but the final work must be your own and based on your own individual opinions, viewpoint and experiences.

Once you have completed the reflection section, submit the final version of your individual report to your teacher to be assessed.

b) Make sure you note and understand the feedback you are given and then set targets for progress in Global Perspectives next year.

Reflecting on your progress

Reflection needs an organised structure.

- How confident are you now in organising your reflections?

- How can you explain the links between what you have learned and how your own perspective has changed?

Let's now revisit the other type of reflection, where you reflect on the development of your own Global Perspectives skills.

2 Look back at your Global Perspectives studies this year.

a) Which issue that you explored most changed the way you think and act?

b) Which of the six skills (Analysis, Collaboration, Communication, Research, Evaluation and Reflection) do you think you now understand much better?

c) How would you demonstrate that you have made progress in this skill?

Discuss your responses with a partner, then share your ideas with the class.

Good reflection needs to be supported by specific examples. You need to link the examples to action or learning that you have done.

3 Working on your own, make some notes about the key turning points in your understanding of an issue you have studied in Global Perspectives this year. The topics you have studied are:

Change in culture and communities	Values and beliefs	Climate change, energy and resources
Migration and urbanisation	Digital world	Law and criminality

a) Give a specific example of learning something new about a topic.

b) Give an example of a global issue about which there are different viewpoints.

c) Give a specific example of how your past thoughts or actions about that issue have developed or changed as a result of something you have learned.

4 Now reflect on your skills development throughout this year's course.

a) Choose two of the Global Perspectives skills.

b) How has your understanding of each of these skills developed in the last year? Give specific examples that demonstrate this.

c) How do the examples prove your points about skills development?

Discuss your responses with a partner, then feed back to the whole class.

5 Make notes on:

a) what you have learned about your individual strengths and weaknesses in applying the Global Perspectives skills

b) how confident you are in reflecting those skills in a written report.

Check your progress

Beginning	Developing	Going beyond
• I can identify national perspectives in news articles and websites.	• I can evaluate different national perspectives in news articles and websites and compare them.	• I can evaluate the reliability and credibility of news articles and websites.
• I can present arguments and discuss how convincing they are.	• I can synthesise different arguments and analyse their strengths and weaknesses.	• I can evaluate how persuasive an argument is in terms of its structure and use of evidence.
• I can present information and opinions to support my own arguments.	• I can present evidence to support my own reasoning.	• I can present information and opinions, referencing sources (both global and local) to support my reasoning.
• I can identify the skills I have practised in my writing and identify my strengths and weaknesses.	• I can reflect on my skills in carrying out an activity, identifying and balancing out strengths and weaknesses.	• I can evaluate how I have developed my skills and identify targets for improvement, relating them directly to what I have learned during an activity.

Next steps

Explore other legal issues in relation to rights and responsibilities online from your own national perspective. What laws could make a difference? Are these proposals you could take forward yourself or encourage others to do?

Think about how you can develop the Global Perspectives skill that you have identified as a weakness. What would help: more writing, more internet research or more help with structuring arguments? Which other curriculum subjects could you use to improve that skill?

Glossary of key terms

analogy: a comparison made between two things in order to explain or clarify

anecdotal evidence: evidence based on people's own experiences

anticipate: to plan for what you think will happen

assertion: a statement presented as fact without supporting evidence

bibliography: a list of books or articles referenced, for example in an essay, report or presentation

collate: to put together and organise, for example research findings or data

consensus: agreement

continuum: line representing a continuous progression from one possibility to an opposing one

correlation: relationship or connection between two or more things

credibility: the extent to which something can be trusted and is believable

credible: believable, convincing

data: facts and statistics (numerical data) gathered for analysis

data set: collection of linked data (information)

embedded: set within

emotive: showing or evoking strong feelings

empathise: understand why someone thinks or feels something

factual evidence: evidence based on facts; data that can be shown to be true

fieldwork: collecting data outside, 'in the field', in a real environment rather than in a lab or classroom; fieldwork can be done by individuals or by groups

hyperlink: electronic link that takes you to another website or online article

inclined: having a tendency towards something

infographic: information displayed in a visually interesting way

key: part of a graph or map that explains the colours and other symbols used

operative clause: part of the resolution that suggests specific actions, whether national or international

perspective: a viewpoint on an issue based on evidence and reasoning

pitch: how high or low the sound of your voice is

pre-ambulatory clause: part of the resolution that explains the causes, consequences and context of the issue

primary source: original material, for example raw data or a first-hand account, such as a diary entry or interview

proactive: acting before a situation happens rather than after it has occurred

quantifiable: can be measured in a scientific way

refute: argue against

reliable: dependable, trustworthy

representative: a small group that is typical of members of the whole group

resolution: firm decision about how to act

sampling: using a representative group of the population for the purposes of research

secondary source: material that draws on and interprets primary sources, such as articles and reports or graphs and tables based on collected data

SMART: Specific, Measurable, Attainable, Realistic, Time-bound

superscript: when a number or letter is raised above the text line, usually in a smaller font, like this [1]

survey: (verb) to measure or to study something in detail; to find out information or different people's views by asking a series of questions

tone: the sound of your voice, which conveys your feelings, for example angry, uncertain

trend: a general development in the way something happens; a pattern in data, in which the numbers change in a similar way

trust: a belief in someone or something

useful: something we can use for some purpose

viewpoint: a person's view without evidence or reasoning

Acknowledgements

Text and figures

We are grateful to the following for permission to reproduce copyright material. In some instances, we have been unable to trace the owners of copyright material, and we would appreciate any information that would enable us to do so.

A screenshot on p.4 from 'Numerical modelling of floating debris in the world's oceans' from *Marine Pollution Bulletin*, Elsevier, Vol. 64, Issue 3, March 2012, pp.653-661, copyright © 2012 Elsevier Ltd. All rights reserved; Extract on p.15 adapted from 'The Qualities of a Good Research Question' by Janet Zepernick, Pittsburg State University, Kaleidoscope Open Course Initiative, http://www.pittstate.edu/. Attribution 4.0 International (CC BY 4.0); Extracts on pp.26 from 'The Climate Change Debate: We look at two different sides of the argument' by Mina Kerr-Lazenby, *Denizen Magazine,* 23/01/2020, https://www.thedenizen.co.nz/culture/the-climate-change-debate/; and https://www.thedenizen.co.nz/about/, copyright © Denizen. Reproduced with permission; Extract and graph on p.27 adapted from 'Polar Bear population' and 'Trends in Polar Bear Subpopulations', WWF Arctic Programme, https://www.arcticwwf.org/wildlife/polar-bear/polar-bear-population/. Reproduced with permission; Extracts on p.28 adapted from 'Conservation concerns' and 'Status', Polar Bears International, https://polarbearsinternational.org. Reproduced with permission; Extracts on p.28 adapted from 'The Myth That the Polar Bear Population Is Declining' by Jon Miltimore, The Foundation for Economic Education (FEE), 09/09/2019 https://fee.org/articles/the-myth-that-the-polar-bear-population-is-declining/ and https://fee.org/about. Reproduced with permission; Data on p.32 adapted from *How Bad Are Bananas* by Mike Berner-Lees, Profile Books, 2020. Reproduced with permission; An extract on p.38 from 'Illegal Hotel El Algarrobico Demolition Action in Spain', Greenpeace, 23/02/2016, https://media.greenpeace.org/archive/Illegal-Hotel-El-Algarrobico-Demolition-Action-in-Spain-27MZIFJ6I1JE8.html. Reproduced with permission; An extract on p.58 from '7 Migrants Share Their Stories of Struggle and Resilience re: Yerima, Togo to Spain' by Joe McCarthy, *Global Citizen*, 29/10/2019, https://www.globalcitizen.org/fr/content/migrant-first-person-stories-undp. Reproduced with permission; An extract on p.59 from '13 Powerful Refugee Stories From Around The World' by Miranda Cleland, *Global Giving*, June 2022, https://www.globalgiving.org/learn/listicle/13-powerful-refugee-stories/, copyright © Middle East Children's Alliance. Reproduced with permission; Statistics on p.60 from *Global Migration Data Portal*; and *Global Migration Indicators 2021*, *Insights from the Global Migration Data Portal* by J. Black, 2021, p.30, source UNESCO, 2021. www.migrationdataportal.org. International Organization for Migration (IOM), Geneva, copyright © IOM GMDAC. Accessed 16/11/2022; The figure on p.63 'Filipino Professional Nurses Deployed Overseas, 2000–2015' adapted from 'Learning to Fill the Labor Niche: Filipino Nursing Graduates and the Risk of the Migration Trap' by Yasmin Y. Ortiga, *RSF: The Russell Sage Foundation Journal of the Social Sciences* Volume 4, Issue 1, eds. Susan Eckstein and Giovanni Peri, copyright © Russell Sage Foundation, 112 East 64th Street, New York, NY 10065, https://www.rsfjournal.org/content/4/1/172. Reproduced with Permission; Data on p.63 adapted from 'A global profile of emigrants to OECD countries: Younger and more skilled migrants from more diverse countries' by R. d'Aiglepierre, et al, *OECD Social, Employment and Migration Working Papers*, No. 239, OECD Publishing Paris, 2020, https://doi.org/10.1787/0cb305d3-en; Map on p.64 from 'Origins and Destinations of the World's Migrants, 1990–2017' Pew Research Center, 28/02/2018, https://www.pewresearch.org/global/interactives/global-migrant-stocks-map/, data source: United Nations Population Division; Data on p.66 from 'Personal Remittances, received (current US$) – Philippines, World Bank, 2016–2020, https://data.worldbank.org/indicator/BX.TRF.PWKR.CD.DT?locations=PH, Creative Commons Attribution 4.0 (CC-BY 4.0); Figure on p.67 from 'Coronavirus Pandemic (Covid 19)' by Edouard Mathieu, Hannah Ritchie, Lucas Rodés-Guirao, Cameron Appel, Daniel Gavrilov, Charlie Giattino, Joe Hasell, Bobbie Macdonald, Saloni Dattani, Diana Beltekian, Esteban Ortiz-Ospina, and Max Roser. Our World in Data, 2020, https://ourworldindata.org/coronavirus. CreativeCommons BY License; An extract on p.106 from "Online Image – How Do We Present Ourselves Online?" by Josh Renyard, 16/05/2019, https://blog.yorksj.ac.uk/joshua-renyard/2019/05/16/online-image-how-do-we-present-ourselves-online/. Reproduced with kind permission; An extract on p.107 from 'The Benefits of Being Yourself Online' by Erica R. Bailey, Sandra Matz, *Scientific American*, 09/02/21, copyright © Scientific American, a Division of Springer Nature America, Inc., 2021. Reproduced with permission. All rights reserved; An extract on p.114 from 'What's Wrong With MOOCs, and Why Aren't They Changing the Game in Education?' by Harman Singh, *Wired*, August 2004, https://www.wired.com/insights/2014/08/whats-wrong-moocs-arent-changing-game-education/. Reproduced with kind permission from the author; An extract and chart on p.115 from 'Who's Benefiting from MOOCs, and Why' by Chen Zhenghao, Brandon Alcorn, Gayle Christensen, Nicholas Eriksson, Daphne Koller, and Ezekiel J. Emanuel, Harvard Business Review, 22/09/2015, copyright © 2015 by the President and Fellows of Harvard College. All Rights Reserved; An extract on p.129 from "'All I can do is wait'": Children make up a third of migrants in documentation limbo' by Athena Ankrah, Cronkite Borderlands Project, 01/08/2022, https://cronkitenews.azpbs.org/2022/08/01/tapachula-mexico-children-migrants-wait-for-immigration-documents-aid/. Reproduced with permission; An extract on p.130 from 'Radio-based learning gets its day in the sun in Mali Solar-powered radios are helping conflict-affected and displaced children follow lessons outside of the classroom' by Fatou Diagne, UNICEF, https://www.unicef.org/stories. Reproduced with permission; and an extract on pp.135–136 from 'We must all stand with #ChildrenUprooted' by Anja Nielsen, UKFIET, 02/12/2019, https://www.ukfiet.org/2019/climate-migration-and-education-are-we-making-our-education-systems-future-proof/. Reproduced with permission from UKFIET, with thanks to UNICEF.

Images

We are grateful for the following for permission to reproduce their images:

p.1 Fabien Monteil/Shutterstock,p.2 Tolu Owoeye/Shutterstock, p.3 MOHAMED ABDULRAHEEM/Shutterstock, p.4 Frances Roberts / Alamy Stock Photo, p.4 David Pereiras/Shutterstock, p.4 Marine Pollution Bulletin, 2012., p.5 SeventyFour/

Shutterstock, p.6 Strahil Dimitrov/Shutterstock, p.6 Andrea Quintero Olivas/Shutterstock, p.8 Monkey Business Images/Shutterstock, p.10 New Africa/Shutterstock, p.13 yerv/Shutterstock, p.15 Wichaiwish/Shutterstock, p.15 Alyoshin E/Shutterstock, p.16 BAO-Images Bildagentur/Shutterstock, p.16 Ashley Cooper/Alamy Stock Photo, p.16 Lost_in_the_Midwest/Shutterstock, p.16 Aleksandr Simonov/Shutterstock, p.17 Lolostock/Shutterstock, p.17 New Africa/Shutterstock, p.17 imageBROKER/Alamy Stock Photo, p.18 [Photographer: John Charles Burrow, c.1900] Contributor:De Luan/Alamy Stock Photo, p.18 Copyright The Francis Frith Collection, p.19 Darling Archive/Alamy Stock Photo, p.20 Radek Sturgolewski/Shutterstock, p.21 J L IMAGES/Shutterstock, p.21 petrmalinak/Shutterstock, p.22 vchal/Shutterstock, p.22 Tasha Vector/Shutterstock, p.23 Demetrio Zimino/Shutterstock, p.24 HollyHarry/Shutterstock, p.25 joerngebhardt68/Shutterstock, p.27 Jan Martin Will/Shutterstock, p.29 Ody_Stocker/Shutterstock, p.30 Flexd Design/Shutterstock, p.31 Olena Yakobchuk/Shutterstock, p.31 ZouZou/Shutterstock, p.33 emileynp/Shutterstock, p.33 Morakot Kawinchan/Shutterstock, p.33 Ground Picture/Shutterstock, p.34 Odua Images/Shutterstock, p.35 thirawatana phaisalratana/Shutterstock, p.37 Vicki L. Miller/Shutterstock, p.38 Kues/Shutterstock, p.38 GP0STPMX6, © Pedro Armestre / Greenpeace, p.39 Magnus Binnerstam/Shutterstock, p.40 michaeljung/Shutterstock, p.42 Marjolein Hameleers/Shutterstock, p.44 Tony Cowburn/Shutterstock, p.45 Juice Verve/Shutterstock, p.46 Khanh Le/Shutterstock, p.47 Roop_Dey/Shutterstock, p.48 Bernard Staehli/Shutterstock, p.49 mrinalpal/Shutterstock, p.50 Atmotu Images/Alamy Stock Photo, p.51 Nick Fox/Shutterstock, p.52 Agus D. Laksono/Alamy Stock Photo, p.52 Esstock/Shutterstock, p.54 Rawpixel Ltd / Alamy Stock Photo, p.55 Monkey Business Images/Shutterstock, p.55 i_am_zews/Shutterstock, p.55 Mazur Travel/Shutterstock, p.57 Yupgi/Shutterstock, p.58 Lena Mucha/UNDP, p.58 Yerima Gado, © Lena Mucha/UNDP, www.lenamucha.com; p.59 Global Giving picture of Shafaq copyright © Middle East Children's Alliance; p.60 F Armstrong Photography/Shutterstock, p.60 Pressmaster/Shutterstock, p.61 WESTOCK PRODUCTIONS/Shutterstock, p.62 By Ian Miles-Flashpoint Pictures/Alamy Stock Photo, p.63 National Archives photo no. 350-P-E-34-8-1. Operating Room – Philippine General Hospital, Manila, P.I. Taken by the Philippine Bureau of Science, Manila, p.65 metamorworks/Shutterstock, p.65 Boyloso/Shutterstock, p.66 The Road Provides/Shutterstock, p.66 GBJSTOCK/Shutterstock, p.66 Hryshchyshen Serhii/Shutterstock, p.68 Vectomart/Shutterstock, p.68 DrimaFilm/Shutterstock, p.68 Rawpixel.com/Shutterstock, p.70 cartoon copyright © Godfrey Mwampembwa (GADO), Buni Media, p.73 WHYFRAME/Shutterstock, p.73 Ibrahim Songne, © Marilena Delli Umuhoza, p.74 Stock Rocket/Shutterstock, p.75 Ground Picture/Shutterstock, p.76 milatas/Shutterstock, p.76 Farid Huseynov/Shutterstock, p.79 TonyV3112/Shutterstock, p.80 BearFotos/Shutterstock, p.81 Markos Loizou/Shutterstock, p.82 Vova Shevchuk/Shutterstock, p.83 apiguide/Shutterstock, p.84 Pises Tungittipokai/Shutterstock, p.85 Rawpixel.com/Shutterstock, p.86 ACHPF/Shutterstock, p.88 miya227/Shutterstock, p.89 Lightfield Studios Inc./Alamy Stock Photo, p.90 milatas/Shutterstock, p.92 New Africa/Shutterstock, p.94 mentatdgt/Shutterstock, p.95 SeventyFour/Shutterstock, p.96 Rawpixel.com/Shutterstock, p.97 sokolfly/Shutterstock, p.98 Lightfield Studios Inc./Shutterstock, p.100 Karolina Krasuska/Alamy Stock Photo, p.101 Sensay/Shutterstock, p.103 Ground Picture/Shutterstock, p.104 Gorodenkoff/Shutterstock, p.105 Supamotion/Shutterstock, p.105 Volha Hlinskaya/Shutterstock, p.105 Krakenimages.com/Shutterstock, p.106 Vergani Fotografia/Shutterstock, p.108 BaLL LunLa/Shutterstock, p.109 Dipendra Lamsal/Shutterstock, p.110 Prathankarnpap/Shutterstock, p.111 LookerStudio/Shutterstock, p.112 Ground Picture/Shutterstock, p.113 Monkey Business Images/Shutterstock, p.116 Miew S/Shutterstock, p.117 Drop of Light/Shutterstock, p.118 Hayk_Shalunts/Shutterstock, p.119 Filip Jedraszak/Shutterstock, p.120 RossHelen/Shutterstock, p.121 zhu difeng/Shutterstock, p.122 Daisy Daisy/Shutterstock, p.122 Sergey Nivens/Shutterstock, p.122 NicoElNino/Shutterstock, p.122 Andrey_Popov/Shutterstock, p.123 ALDECA studio/Shutterstock, p.124 Anton Vierietin/Shutterstock, p.127 SuperStock/Alamy Stock Photo, p.128 Rawpixel.com/Shutterstock, p.129 copyright © Juliette Rihl, Cronkite Borderlands Project, p.132 Alexandros Michailidis/Shutterstock, p.134 Drop of Light/Shutterstock, p.135 bodom/Shutterstock, p.137 chrisdorney/Shutterstock, p.138 lev radin/Shutterstock, p.141 milatas/Shutterstock, p.142 Jacob Lund/Shutterstock, p.143 John Wreford/Shutterstock, p.144 Tom Wang/Shutterstock, p.145 Wirestock Creators/Shutterstock, p.146 metamorworks/Shutterstock, p.148 Gonzalo Bell/Shutterstock, p.149 Drazen Zigic/Shutterstock.

In some instances, we have been unable to trace the owners of copyright material, and we would appreciate any information that would enable us to do so.